Advance Praise for

Puzzles, Paradoxes, Controversies, and the Global Economy

"*Puzzles, Paradoxes, Controversies, and the Global Economy* is Charlie Wolf at his best. On a breathtaking array of subjects, from China's growth to macroeconomic theory and policy, from geopolitics to public debate over decline and inequality, Wolf is always insightful and stimulating, usually provocative, often contrarian. Read from cover to cover or separate chapters one at a time, you are in for fresh perspectives on vital and timeless issues."

Michael J. Boskin, Tully M. Friedman Professor of Economics and Hoover Institution senior fellow, Stanford University, and former chairman, President's Council of Economic Advisers

"Ranging across topics as diverse as income inequality, energy policy, and foreign aid, Charles Wolf distills complex economic arguments into compelling prose while linking them to broader geopolitical currents."

Henry A. Kissinger, former secretary of state (1973–77) and former national security adviser (1969–75)

"Charles Wolf has produced a masterful review of the most salient economic issues of the coming era. Rightly centered on China's rise but not limited to it, he makes a convincing case that America's prosperity will depend on our finding the right strategy in a world very different from the one we have known."

Henry Rowen, professor emeritus of Stanford University at the Graduate School of Business and the Asia/Pacific Research Center of the Freeman-Spogli Institute for International Studies, and a senior fellow at the Hoover Institution

"Charlie Wolf writes with clarity, concision, and common sense about an extraordinary range of domestic and international policy issues. For anyone interested in China's economy and its interactions with the US and the wider world, or the record of Keynesian remedies for what ails American growth, or the sources of and palliatives for inequality in a growing number of countries, or the future of the dollar and yuan, this is a volume of essays to treasure."

Michael Armacost, former US ambassador to Japan and the Philippines

Puzzles, Paradoxes,
Controversies,
and the Global Economy

Puzzles, Paradoxes, Controversies, and the Global Economy

Charles Wolf Jr.

HOOVER INSTITUTION PRESS
Stanford University   Stanford, California

www.hoover.org

Hoover Institution Press Publication No. 659

Hoover Institution at Leland Stanford Junior University, Stanford, California 94305-6010

First printing 2015
22   21   20   19   18   17   16   15   9 8 7 6 5 4 3 2 1

Manufactured in the United States of America

The paper used in this publication meets the minimum Requirements of the American National Standard for Information Sciences—Permanence of Paper for Printed Library Materials, ANSI/NISO Z39.48-1992. ♾

Cataloging-in-Publication Data is available from the Library of Congress.
ISBN: 978-0-8179-1855-2 (pbk. : alk. paper)
ISBN: 978-0-8179-1856-9 (epub)
ISBN: 978-0-8179-1857-6 (mobi)
ISBN: 978-0-8179-1858-3 (PDF)

For Theresa, an unopinionated lady possessed of strong opinions:
when she rereads these chapters, she will probably
agree with fewer than half

Contents

Foreword

Charlie Wolf combines two gifts that seldom go together: an original mind and the ability to write clear English sentences in logical order. Some people have one or the other of these two talents, but Charlie was blessed with both.

Charlie's essays cover the waterfront, from China's economy, to the US economy, to the economies of Japan, Korea, and India—the works. Years ago, I served as a trustee and later chairman of the RAND Corporation and often heard him brief our board and staff. One day I suggested to Charlie that he put his thoughts into essays and op-eds so that they could be shared with a wider audience. The result: dozens of Charlie's works were published in the *Wall Street Journal, Forbes,* the *South China Morning Post,* and the *Weekly Standard.* Putting them into a single volume, along with two essays not yet published elsewhere, enables the reader to absorb his perspective over the years. Charlie believes that the collection exceeds the sum of its parts. As usual, he is right.

Newton N. Minow
Senior Counsel, Sidley Austin LLP

Preface

The chapters in this book were written between 2007 and the first half of 2014. Several chapters summarize published work done at RAND during this period. Other chapters resulted from further thoughts about what was covered in the RAND work, while a few others were prompted by thoughts about what was *not* in that work. Many of the chapters are not directly related to my RAND work or are only remotely related to it. Thirty-five of the thirty-seven chapters were previously published as op-eds in the *Wall Street Journal, Forbes,* and *South China Morning Post* or as lengthier essays in the *Weekly Standard,* in journals previously published by the Hoover Institution, as a book chapter (published by Routledge), or as brief responses to specific questions raised by symposia published in the *International Economy.* Two chapters were previously unpublished: Chapter 14 (dealing with puzzles about the US economy's pallid recovery from the 2008 recession) and Chapter 26 (suggesting that bipartisanship in the US Congress—while refreshing and laudable for its own sake—may not lead to sensible policy).

Collecting the separate essays in a single volume makes them more accessible. More importantly, the collection may exceed the sum of its parts. That excess includes a few broad themes that are latent in individual chapters but emerge more clearly when they're repeated and amplified in several chapters. One such theme is the paradoxes and puzzles within China's political economy and in its interactions with the United States. Another broad theme—more resonant in the United States, Europe, and Japan than in China—is the validity or, as I contend in several chapters, the shortcomings of Keynesian economics as a guide to designing appropriate policies (i.e., "fiscal stimulus" and "monetary easing") for responding to the recession of 2008 and recovering from it. Part of this theme consists of pointing out the shortcomings of Keynesian theory. Another part relates to shortcomings of policies and actions inferred from the theory.

A third theme that links several chapters is economic inequality—its scale in the United States, China, Europe, Japan, and other countries, both pretax and post-tax—and whether its principal sources lie in unequal productivity among different investments, different economic sectors, and different segments of the labor force or instead lie in cronyism, nepotism, and other corruptive influences. Remedies or palliatives for inequality differ greatly depending on its principal sources.

Another theme spans four chapters focused on China's currency and the continuing controversy about whether and when it may become a major international reserve currency and, in the interim, whether the renminbi's exchange rate is more likely to depreciate (as I suggest) or appreciate (as contended by the US Treasury Department and by some members of the US Congress).

The chapters differ widely in length—several thousand words for book chapters and book summaries but only a few hundred words in response to specific issues or questions posed by symposia periodically conducted by the *International Economy*. These differences may enable readers to choose among the chapters according to their available time, patience, and interest in the subject.

I have long believed that media commentators, as well as academics and officials, who opine profusely on many issues, ought to be accountable through some means of assessing the validity and mistakes of their prior opinions. Whether this assessment is provided by the judgments of fair-minded others, by the authors themselves, or preferably by both, an attempt at accountability would help raise the level of public debate and enhance future credibility. With this in mind, I append at the end of each chapter a "Postaudit," representing my subjective assessment of the chapter's content: "good," "medium," or "not good." The terms are more or less self-explanatory. If the chapter contains or implies a forecast, the evaluation indicates whether the forecast turned out to be accurate, or at least still appears accurate in light of the intervening years' further evidence, or has been found to be wide of the mark. If the chapter does not contain an explicit forecast, the assessment is intended to indicate whether the chapter seems to be as relevant now as it was when I wrote it. The bottom line, according to my perhaps biased assessment: 76 percent seem "good"; 19 percent "medium" (or ambiguous); 5 percent "not good."

In classes I teach in the Pardee RAND Graduate School and have taught elsewhere in the past, I haven't been considered a particularly generous grader. But maybe my subjective assessments are marred by indulgent self-generosity compared with assessments I've accorded to others. In any event, readers are invited to make their own assessments and especially invited to let me know whether and why theirs differ from mine.

Charles Wolf Jr.
November 2014

Acknowledgments

It is a pleasure to express my appreciation to the following people for their invaluable assistance in completing this book: Fatima Ford, my assistant at RAND, for diligence in locating, organizing, and assembling the component parts; Rebecca Logan, at Newgen, for correcting, proofing, and standardizing the frequent vagaries of prior publications; Barbara Arellano, at Stanford's Hoover Institution Press, for admirable efficiency in managing, scheduling, and tracking the publication process; and finally, John Raisian, director of the Hoover Institution, for encouraging and supporting this second iteration of a project whose predecessor, *Looking Backward and Forward: Policy Issues in the Twenty-first Century,* was published by Hoover in 2008.

PART I

China's Economy

1 The Paradoxes of China

China, on the cusp of a major leadership transition, has cropped up only sporadically in our presidential campaign. The candidates, in their occasional comments on our largest lender and trading partner, seem to vie with one another only in how tough each will be. But toughness is not a policy.

China is rife with paradoxes. They include paradoxes of class, foreign aid, military spending, and corruption. Whether and how they are resolved will seriously affect the evolution of policies within China, as well as its future relations with the United States.

The Class Paradox

In principle and doctrine (Mao, Marx), communism in China aspires to a classless society. In practice, it is formally stratified into a multitiered hierarchy of specified classes. The twenty-seven tiers encompass not only government officialdom but the Communist Party of China's eighty-three million members as well: at the middle and higher levels, most government officials

This chapter was previously published as Charles Wolf Jr., "The Paradoxes of China," *Weekly Standard*, November 5, 2012, http://www.weeklystandard.com /articles/paradoxes-china_657942.html#.

are also CPC members. The defined classes extend to state-owned enterprises (SOEs), the military's upper reaches, and such public services and nongovernmental organizations as hospitals, schools, and research institutes. Because Jiang Zemin called for eligibility for CPC membership to be extended to businessmen and businesswomen, the stratification encompasses some from the private sector as well.

The steps on the stratification ladder are differentiated in several ways. Compensation levels vary widely, consisting of an explicit "visible" component and a substantially larger "invisible" component, including different allowances, benefits, and other perquisites. For the visible component, the spread between top and bottom is a modest tenfold; for the invisible component, it is probably several orders of magnitude—that is, a thousand or more times—larger.

The classes are also sharply differentiated by the honorific conferrals that accompany them. The rarefied top reach of Class 1 is thinly populated by the party general secretary (who also is China's president and chairman of its Central Military Commission) and several of the other eight members of the Politburo Standing Committee, including the premier and the chairman of the National People's Congress. Class 2 includes the vice president and deputy premier, other members of the Politburo, and the first vice-chairman of the People's Congress. Classes 3 and 4 include members of the Central Committee and the State Council, and governors of major provinces and of megacities like Beijing, Shanghai, and Chongqing. As a rough approximation, these top four classes correspond to what was referred to in the bygone Soviet Union as its *nomenklatura;* in China, they have some of the trappings of royalty.

China's remaining classes are filled in descending order by government leaders of smaller provinces and cities and by the lower-level officials and CPC cadres who occupy the remaining tiers of the class pyramid.

The system provides for meritocratic mobility among the classes, although an element of legacy intrudes in this process. For example, the so-called princelings—children and relatives of previous top-tier leaders—often inherit upscale status quite apart from their merit. The recent Bo Xilai–Gu Kailai–Wang Lijun scandal in Chongqing was replete with evidence of the legacy phenomenon.

How the paradox of a sharply stratified class structure juxtaposed with a principled doctrine of classlessness will resonate in an extensively networked and increasingly informed population of 1.3 billion people is a high-stakes "riddle wrapped in a mystery inside an enigma," as Winston Churchill once said about Russia.

The Foreign Aid Paradox

In recent years, China's annual worldwide foreign aid has been very large (more than China's officially reported defense budgets), concentrated on development of natural resources (fossil fuels, ferrous and nonferrous metals), and extended to ninety-three countries with exacting, quid pro quo conditions attached to the loans that require repayment in kind and thus accord with the direct economic interests of the donor. Hence, China's aid has a distinctly "capitalist" character, in contrast to the more "philanthropic" aid extended by the "capitalist" West.

Development of natural resources made up nearly 40 percent of the pledged totals, infrastructure development amounted to 45 percent, and the remaining 15 percent consisted of technical assistance, humanitarian aid, education aid, and recipients' sovereign debt acquired or forgiven by China.

Most of this aid is financed by subsidized loans from the China Development Bank, its Export-Import Bank, and the China-Africa

Development Fund. These sources are supplemented by technical and financial support from major SOEs that have natural resource development interests. Formal management responsibility for China's foreign aid resides in the Ministry of Commerce.

Loan agreements accompanying foreign aid projects typically stipulate that commodities produced by the natural resource projects will be exported to China, that the lending institutions establish escrow accounts into which the revenues from these exports will be deposited, and that the lending institutions withdraw interest and principal for debt servicing and for fees and other payments due to contractors from these escrow accounts.

The paradox of China's foreign aid is that, unlike traditional, philanthropic aid provided by the capitalistic United States, European Union, and Japan, the quid pro quo transactional conditions attached to China's foreign aid projects are distinctly capitalistic.

The Military Spending Paradox

To frame the military spending paradox, two points are crucial: the first is the special meanings that "liberal" and "conservative" have in China; the second is the pace of military spending growth in China.

"Liberals" in China are those who favor economic reform with a dominant role for market-based pricing and market-based resource allocation and who seek to reduce central planning and government control. "Conservatives," on the other hand, favor increased reliance on state enterprise, central planning, and protectionism and diminished reliance on markets.

During the first decade of the twenty-first century, China's real gross domestic product increased at an average annual rate of 10.2 percent, while real military spending increased at an average annual rate of 12.1 percent; both rates were the highest among all the world's major economies, and the substantially higher rate of military spending growth was unique to China.

China's liberals endorse the growth of military spending no less enthusiastically than do China's conservatives. Indeed, China's liberals view rapid increases in peacetime military spending as an essential part of economic reform, distinguishing them from the liberals of the Western world, who press for lower levels of military spending and for lower rates of growth in peacetime military spending.

The Corruption Paradox

Members and adherents of the CPC confront two sharply divergent views of corruption—defined as officialdom's use of public authority to extract personal profit at the expense of the public good.

Mao Zedong viewed the practice permissively, if not dismissively. He analogized strict efforts at curtailing corruption to trying to "squeeze out all the toothpaste" from the tube: not likely to succeed and not worth the effort. At moderate levels, he viewed it as a peccadillo and perhaps a lubricant for the smooth functioning of the system. According to Mao, "Among those whose labor is good, no (corrupt) label should be given," and rehabilitation should be quick and easy.

A sharply different view is advanced by others, including some in the upper levels of the hierarchy referred to in the above discussion of the class paradox. They see the conspicuous rise in corruption as a threat to the party's "legitimacy" and its continued monopoly on political power. Furthermore, some of those holding this view worry that as long as the state plays a major role in the economy, corruption will grow. Consequently, they favor greater reliance on the private sector, freer markets, and sharp reductions in the state's economic power.

The paradoxes that pervade the China scene are deep, abiding, and in some cases, counterintuitive to Western thinking. Still, when it comes to assessing the complexities of US-China relations, the paradoxes should be an important part of the calculus—indeed, more important than reiterated "toughness."

POSTAUDIT

Although this article was written in 2012, the paradoxes are undiminished in 2014; still other paradoxes could be added to the ones cited in the article—for example, China's aging demographic versus its "one-child" family and China's growing frustration with North Korea, even though North Korea is more dependent on China. *Score: Good*

---

2 China's Expanding Role in Global Merger-and-Acquisition Markets

Summary

CHARLES WOLF JR., BRIAN G. CHOW,
GREGORY S. JONES, AND SCOTT HAROLD

Background and Scope

One of the few propositions on which virtually all China experts agree is that foreign investment *in* China has been a major contributor to the Chinese economy's remarkable growth over the past three decades. In addition to the direct benefits realized from the invested capital itself—which increased more than sixfold between 1992 and 2007—significant additional benefits accrued indirectly from the technology, management, and marketing skills that were associated with foreign investment.

From China's perspective, these large capital inflows were sometimes viewed as entailing risks that were mitigated by imposing restrictions on foreign investment. These measures included limiting foreign equity investment to nonvoting Class B shares, constraining the proportion of ownership that foreign investors could acquire in Chinese companies, and limiting the number and size of foreign firms' financial platforms in China's capital markets.

This chapter was previously published as Charles Wolf Jr., Brian G. Chow, Gregory S. Jones, and Scott Harold, "Summary," in *China's Expanding Role in Global Mergers and Acquisitions Markets* (Santa Monica, CA: RAND, 2011), ix–xviii.

In the coming decade, foreign investments *by* China may become an important contributor to growth in the rest of the world and a major factor in global merger-and-acquisition markets. Besides the direct effects of prospective investments from China, there also will be indirect benefits realized through improved know-how, learning, and market access relating to local procedures and regulations within China's thirty-seven diverse provinces and administrative regions. From the perspectives of recipients of China's foreign investments, there may also be concerns and risks. These risks may entail the broad national interests, sensitive technologies, and natural resources of countries receiving China's investments. Recipient countries may thus seek to mitigate these risks through various measures discussed in this chapter.

In this chapter, we seek to improve understanding of China's foreign investment patterns and strategy. We explicitly consider whether and how US national interests might be compromised by some of China's investments and how these interests can be safeguarded without interfering with, indeed by encouraging, opportunities for investments that advance the economic interests of the United States, other countries, and China.

Our research focused on China's investments in US companies and, more particularly, investments in US companies whose acquisition by China might affect US national security. This focus entailed paying special attention to prior investments by China that led to reviews by the United States and to potential investments that might warrant such assessments in the future. The research also sought to compare China's investments in the United States with those of several top-rated private equity (PE) companies to provide a benchmark for evaluating their respective similarities and differences, as well as their patterns and inferred priorities. A fuller understanding of China's investment strategy also required looking more broadly at China's investments in countries other than the United States and considering how China's investments in the United States fit into this broader pattern. Consequently, the research described in this chapter also provides an initial examination of the pattern of China's investments in Europe, Asia, and the rest of the world and inferences that may be drawn from this wider view of China's foreign investment strategy.

China, the United States, and the Global Economy

In the evolving global economy, China's large and growing financial resources will strengthen its bargaining power when it looks for companies and resources abroad. The resulting challenge for both target investment countries and China is how to nurture the opportunities for and potential benefits from efficient allocation of Chinese investments while avoiding or sharply limiting possible risks to national security in the countries of proposed investments. The implied goal of this research is to develop policies and procedures that will promote win-win outcomes while minimizing outcomes that might involve losses for the countries involved.

The drivers of China's remarkable economic growth during the past three decades have included both direct investment from abroad and massive domestic investment constituting more than 35 percent of China's gross domestic product (GDP), an unprecedentedly high domestic savings rate of 45 percent of GDP, continued growth of labor productivity and total factor productivity, and open and expanding markets for China's exports, especially to the United States until mid-2008. These drivers have also included important institutional changes in China: privatization of state-owned enterprises, vigorously competitive domestic product markets, volatile and sometimes highly speculative securities markets, emergent attention to corporate governance, and serious if imperfectly effective efforts to control corruption.

As a consequence of these multiple drivers, China has become the world's second-largest economy. As its economy has grown,

China has accumulated the world's largest holdings of foreign exchange reserves—over $2.1 trillion at the start of 2010, one-third larger than those of Japan. These huge holdings enable China to expand its foreign investments and to seek and acquire companies and other assets abroad.

China's increased prominence in the evolving global economy also stems from its bilateral economic relations with the United States; the effects of the global financial crisis on these relations, including the respective fiscal stimulus programs in China and the United States; and the consequences of these matters for China's recent and prospective investments in US companies and in countries and companies in other parts of the world. China's increasing prominence in the world economy has led to some discussion of possible reforms to the international financial system in which the yuan would become a generally accepted international reserve currency. Such reforms are unlikely in the short to medium term because the yuan's prospects as a reserve currency are remote as long as it remains incompletely convertible. China's policy makers have repeatedly stipulated that capital transactions are unlikely to be fully convertible for the indefinite future. In the longer run, the prospects are brighter.

China's Recent and Prospective Foreign Investments

China's broad foreign investment strategy appears to be distinctive, selective, and flexible.

It is distinctive in that it reflects both the central government and ruling party's broad national priorities that prominently include the salient need of the Chinese economy to sustain high rates of economic growth. This distinctive role of the central government results from the fact that China's major foreign capital transactions require approval of the State Assets Board (SAB) and the State Administration for Foreign Exchange (SAFE), which are accountable to the State Council. When competing claims arise for using China's foreign investments to help meet the demands of the economy, the military, or the economy's technological advancement, these claims are resolved by the institutions at the top of the institutional pyramid. The distinctiveness of China's investment strategy is also reflected in the contrast between Chinese investments in recent years and investments made in the same period by several prominent global PE firms: Blackstone, Kohlberg-Kravis-Roberts, Carlyle, Cerberus, and Berkshire Hathaway.

That China's investment strategy is selective is evident from the conspicuous differences between China's investments in the United States and its investments in Europe, Asia, and the rest of the world during 2007–2009. Selectivity is also reflected by the fact that China's foreign investments sometimes focus on realizing stable returns or realizing higher if more volatile returns, whereas in other instances, the focus is on acquiring companies with large oil, gas, and other mineral resource holdings or companies with advanced technology, laboratories, and testing capabilities. In still other instances, the companies China has acquired are ones with evident financial experience, connections, and know-how.

That the strategy is flexible is suggested by recent policy pronouncements by top Chinese leaders expressing encouragement for expanded Chinese investment abroad, especially by China's most "capable" companies, including state-owned enterprises, while adopting a more restrictive stance toward ones judged less capable.

Notwithstanding frequent Chinese criticism of mounting US budget deficits and the jeopardy this creates for the stability of the US dollar, China's investments in the United States continue to be predominantly in US Treasury notes and bills and other government obligations. China's accumulation of these government assets by the middle of 2009 reached $1.5 trillion, of which nearly one-third was accumulated from 2007 through the middle of 2009. China's investments in US companies in the same period were small, amounting to $25.8 billion, and were concentrated in the financial and business services fields. The reasons for this concentration include China's (plausible but mistaken) expectation of high rates of return on investments in these sectors and the reasonable expectation by China's policy makers that such acquisitions would provide an opportunity to learn about and to access information on the broadest spectrum of companies throughout the US economy.

We expect the scale of China's investments in US companies to rise in the next few years and the pattern to shift from finance and business services. The reasons for this forecast include China's continued accumulation of large current account surpluses, emergent opportunities for acquiring a wider range of US companies as a result of their depressed valuations, the expanding needs of the Chinese economy for high technology, and a growing belief in China that receptivity in the United States to acquisitions by financially well-endowed Chinese investors may be somewhat higher than in prior years.

Our comparison of China's investments in US companies with investments made by the selected PE firms highlights the sharp differences in their respective investment patterns. For example, the five PE firms as a group invested most heavily in hotels and motels, real estate, construction materials, motor vehicles, and packaged frozen foods during the 2007–2009 Great Recession. In sharp contrast, Chinese investments in the same period were concentrated in financial and business services, with smaller stakes in electronics, telecommunications, and medical equipment. In turn, the differing investment patterns reflect the differing business models and differing objectives attributed to each: for China, seeking to meet the expanding needs associated with its aggressive growth and geostrategic interests; for the PE firms, seeking to acquire, enhance, and resell companies at high rates of return in the short to medium term.

Turning to China's investments in Europe in 2007–2009, we have made only an initial, cursory effort to collect and analyze the data. We find that China's investments in Europe concentrated in two sectors during that period: minority acquisitions in multinational oil and gas companies and in financial and banking services. The focus on oil and gas reflects the priority accorded to "resource security" by China's policy makers—a theme that is also dominant in China's investments in Asia and the rest of the world. However, in the European context, the oil and gas priority takes the form of acquiring minority shares in some of the large global multinational producers, whereas in Asia and the rest of the world, the same priority leads to investments aimed at acquiring either full ownership stakes or major stakes in production companies.

We also expect China's investments in Europe to expand as a consequence of China's continuing large current account surpluses. The broadened scope of China's European investments may be affected as well by China's anticipation that acquisitions of high-technology companies may have less sensitivity and encounter less resistance than similarly targeted acquisitions in the United States.

China's investments in Asia and the rest of the world show a markedly different pattern from its investments in the United States and Europe. In Asia and the rest of the world, China's investments have concentrated on resource industries, such as oil, gas, copper, iron, lead, and zinc. Moreover, the small, $18 billion Chinese investment in Asia and the rest of the world in the 2007–2009 period tracked in our study excludes substantial lending ($35 billion) by Chinese financial institutions to resource industries in Brazil and Singapore and additional long-term procurement contracts in Iran and Libya for oil and gas and other resources. These financial commitments may, in some instances, lead to investment acquisitions in the future.

The increasing emphasis on resource investments in these areas is likely to continue in the coming years and grow in scale.

It is not clear whether this policy is wise or optimal, for reasons on both sides of this issue that are discussed more fully below.

Assessing Proposed or Potential Chinese Investments in Other Countries

In considering the effects of foreign investments in the United States, we employ a broad definition of these terms that includes those technologies and services pertinent to economic security and economic growth, not limiting these definitions to the traditional and narrower meanings related to national defense. To develop the methodology, we reviewed twenty proposed Chinese investments from 2000 to 2008 and then refined the design by considering four additional cases to illustrate the framework. We then developed a way to assess the broader national security implications of possible future Chinese investments in financial and business services and in energy.[1]

The analytic methodology, schematized in Figure 2.1, consists of a modified decision-tree analysis involving steps sometimes considered simultaneously, other times considered sequentially.

As the schematic suggests, the methodology describes a process whose successive steps enable the criticality of technology acquisitions to be judged and also shows the status of the potential acquirer to be assessed, whether a national security risk is thereby entailed, whether a mitigation plan can abate such risk, and whether the potential acquirer would have ready access to alternatives to accomplish the same purposes as sought from the acquisition under review.

This process also results in certain guidelines for assessing possible future bids and proposals by China. In developing these guidelines, we invoke the principle of reciprocity between China's treatment of foreign investments in China and potential treatment by other countries of China's investments in them. We

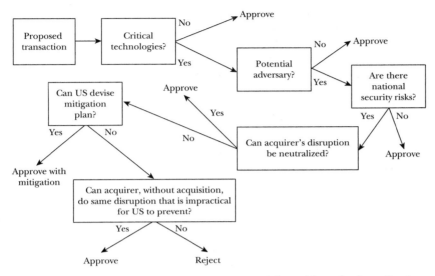

Figure 2.1   Steps for assessing national security risks and benefits from foreign investments

suggest that reciprocity can be invoked without compromising a general preference for open and competitive capital markets. Furthermore, the assessment of risks should be accompanied by a separate assessment of potential benefits from any such acquisition, examining the associated benefits in light of the broadened definition of critical technologies referred to above.

Conclusions, Implications, and Guidelines for Further Research

In the evolving world economy, China's large and growing financial resources are propelled by the world's largest trade balances and the largest current account balances—trends that may diminish somewhat but are likely to continue during the next half-dozen years or more. The result will increase China's influence in the global economy and strengthen its bargaining power as it seeks companies and resources abroad, including those in the United States.

As both a consequence of and contributor to these trends, China's attempts and success in making additional investments in US companies are likely to grow substantially in the coming years. Most of its acquisitions are likely to be mutually beneficial to the United States and to China. Where they may not be beneficial, the analytic methodology we have developed can help to improve understanding and to provide guidelines for further investigation and analysis of such acquisitions.

From discussions within the United States and with China, we concluded that it is important to recall and to invoke the principle of reciprocity in devising mitigation plans to arrive at win-win outcomes and avoid losses to either party. During the past two decades, China has acquired considerable experience in both encouraging and circumscribing foreign, including US, investments in China. Reciprocity would require cooperative and compliant response by China to creative mitigation plans by the United States or other countries for any proposed acquisitions of companies that may entail potential security risks.

Finally, a "wider-angle lens" would be valuable in tracking China's foreign investments. China's investments in European companies should be viewed with a lens that is no less acute than the one applied to viewing China's acquisition of US companies. This also applies to China's investments in Asia and in the rest of the world. In recent years, these investments have mainly been in resource industries, including oil, gas, copper, iron, lead, and zinc. In turn, China's focus on "resource security" is viewed within China as deriving from the high priority that China accords to economic growth and its presumed requirement for secure supplies of critical materials. The wisdom of this policy is open to serious questions, which we address in this chapter. Also open to question is whether China's efforts to expand such investments in Asia and the rest of the world may be as likely to benefit as they are to harm the United States as another principal importer of oil, gas, copper, iron, lead, and zinc. The wider-angle lens for viewing China's investment acquisitions in resource fields can also help anticipate whether and when a series of Chinese investments might lead to acquisition of quasi-monopoly power over valuable ores and other resources, which, in turn, might create vulnerabilities for the economy and national security in the United States and other countries.

Note

1. Other sectors can be examined using the same analytic framework.

POSTAUDIT

This RAND study done in 2010–2011 forecasted increased foreign investments by China in corporate assets abroad, with China continuing but reducing purchases of US government securities. These forecasts are on the mark. *Score: Good*

3   China's Next Buying Spree

Foreign Companies

From 2007 through the first half of this year, Chinese buyers—state, private, and in-between—acquired four hundred companies located outside the country. The acquisitions span a wide range: mining companies in Australia, Vietnam, and South America; oil and gas companies in Africa and the Middle East; banking, financial services, and insurance companies in Europe; and electronics, telecommunications, and lab testing companies in the United States. The total cost? $86 billion.

That may sound like a big number, but in fact it's relatively small. The number of companies at play in global cross-border merger-and-acquisition (M&A) markets during this period exceeded 12,400, with acquisition costs of more than $1.3 trillion. China's share of the total number was 3.2 percent, and its share of total acquisition value was 6.6 percent. China ranks sixth in both number of deals and in acquisition value: behind the United States, United Kingdom, France, Germany, and Japan, though just ahead of the United Arab Emirates. Cross-border acquisitions by US

This article was previously published as Charles Wolf Jr., "China's Next Buying Spree: Foreign Companies," *Wall Street Journal,* January 24, 2011, http://online.wsj.com/articles/SB10001424052748704754304576095880533686442.

investors numbered over 5,000 (42.1 percent of all transactions), and nearly $400 billion by value (30.1 percent of aggregate value).

China's acquisitions beyond its borders are also modest compared with foreign investors' acquisitions within China. Currently, China's annual cross-border acquisitions are about half of annual foreign direct investments in the country.

What is significant about China's acquisitions over the past few years is the change they represent from the negligible amounts in the past. Prior to 2007, nearly all China's foreign investments involved buying US debt, along with lesser purchases of euro and yen debt. China currently holds more than $1.6 trillion of US government debt and an additional $1 trillion of non-US government debt and other assets.

It didn't used to be in the business of acquiring foreign companies. That's changed, and I expect that China's acquisitions will at least double in the next five years and perhaps quadruple by 2020.

There are three principal drivers behind this forecast. First is China's extraordinarily high rate of domestic savings—above 45 percent of gross domestic product (GDP). As long as this rate appreciably exceeds China's not-quite-so-high rate of domestic investment (about 35 percent of GDP), China will have a large global trade surplus, regardless of fluctuations in its exchange rate. This surplus, together with China's net receipts from other sources—including earnings from its prior foreign investments, the excess of inbound versus outbound investment, and remittances from Chinese residents abroad—will generate a current account surplus of $300 billion to $350 billion annually. This will provide a ready source of financing for foreign acquisitions.

Second, China has shifted its focus away from investing in US government debt. While it will continue to invest in such holdings, the investments will be much smaller than in the past. China is aiming to strengthen the renminbi's role as a potential international reserve, thus it will be less willing to shore up the dollar by purchasing large amounts of US government debt. The result is that it will use its surplus to acquire foreign companies.

The third and perhaps strongest driver of a growing Chinese role in international M&A markets is Beijing's interest in acquiring foreign companies that possess one or more of the following characteristics: rich holdings of natural resources, high technology or emergent technologies, and financial know-how and close connections with other financial institutions. Because of the recession, such acquisitions may be available at more attractive prices than usual.

If this forecast is accurate, it will have significant consequences for China and global markets.

Externally, China will be a more active and influential player in global M&A markets. In some cases, China may exercise its financial leverage to successfully challenge competing bidders from other dominant countries. This competition could help integrate China more fully into the global economy.

China's prominence could also lead to increased tension with host countries, especially in light of the marked disparities between the restrictions that it imposes on foreign investors' acquisitions within China and the looser ones usually applied on China's acquisitions abroad. Demands for equivalent and reciprocal treatment shouldn't come as a surprise.

Yet such demands can be expected to evoke strong resistance within China, especially if reciprocal treatment is sought in fields like energy, natural resources, rare earths, chemicals, and infrastructure that are dominated by large state-owned companies such as Sinopec (China Petroleum Company), CNOOC (China National Offshore Oil Corporation), and Sinochem (China Chemical Company).

China's foreign acquisitions will have other repercussions within China. Experience gained from corporate governance in companies it acquires abroad may be a good influence on the often obscure governance practices of Chinese companies. More diligent governance practices—like independent audits and transparent executive compensation—are likely to be met with favor from China's Securities Regulatory Commission but resistance from corporate management. But if the more advanced governance practices prevail, it would be beneficial for China and the rest of the world.

POSTAUDIT

This article, written in 2011, distills a prior RAND study (summarized in Chapter 2) while adding what turns out to be a generally accurate forecast of China's substantial acquisition of foreign commercial assets in the medium (five–six years) term. *Score: Good*

4 China's Foreign Aid and Government-Sponsored Investment Activities

Scale, Content, Destinations, and Implications: Summary

CHARLES WOLF JR., XIAO WANG, AND ERIC WARNER

In the first decade of the twenty-first century, China greatly expanded the scope of its development-assistance and government investment programs. These programs now support initiatives in more than ninety nations around the world. Yet until recently, little was known about the size and direction of such programs. Thomas Lum of the Congressional Research Service offered an initial estimate of the scope and purpose of China's aid and government-sponsored investment activities in Africa, Latin America, and Southeast Asia.[1] In this chapter, we expand on those findings, assessing the scale, trends, and composition of China's foreign aid and government-sponsored investment activities (FAGIA) in Africa, Latin America, the Middle East, South Asia, Central Asia, and East Asia.

We find such programs have burgeoned in recent years and emphasize increasing foreign supplies of energy resources and

This article was previously published as Charles Wolf Jr., Xiao Wang, and Eric Warner, "Summary," in *China's Foreign Aid and Government-Sponsored Investment Activities: Scale, Content, Destinations, and Implications* (Santa Monica, CA: RAND, 2013), xi–xvi.

supplies of ferrous and nonferrous minerals. Loans finance many of these programs and feature substantial subsidization but are also accompanied by rigorous debt-servicing conditions that distinguish China's foreign aid from the grant financing that characterizes development aid provided by the United States and other nations of the Organisation for Economic Co-operation and Development.

Defining China's FAGIA Structure and Size

As we consider it, China's FAGIA are broader than development-assistance programs conducted by the United States and other nations. Official Chinese sources explicitly distinguish three categories of FAGIA: grants, interest-free loans, and concessional loans. The first two are funded by China's state finances, while the Export-Import Bank of China funds the third. Many of these programs fall below the grant element of at least 25 percent that characterizes foreign aid programs of other nations and also have requirements that goods purchased for them be at least 50 percent Chinese origin.

Prior to 2000, China's FAGIA were distinctly limited in scale and content, as, indeed, was China's role in the global economy. Since then, several contributors have reshaped the scale, content, and destinations of this aid. As a result of its remarkable and sustained economic growth, China's shares of global trade and global product increased, as did the resources available to expand its FAGIA. Because future growth of the Chinese economy depends on increasing supplies of natural resources, especially energy-related resources, much of China's assistance has sought to help countries developing such resources.

The financial muscle of China's aid is mainly provided by large loans from China's Export-Import Bank, the China Development Bank, and the China-Africa Development Fund (which is within the CDB). Several state-owned enterprises, including China National Offshore Oil Corporation, the China National Petroleum Corporation, and the China Petrochemical Company, provide technical and financial support. The FAGIA formal management structure is topped by the Ministry of Commerce, which is responsible to China's State Council and ultimately to the Standing Committee of the Communist Party's Political Bureau, the pinnacle of decision-making power in China. Much remains unknown about this structure, including the precise role of the major state-owned enterprises in the planning, decision making, and operation of China's programs; how independently the CDB operates in providing aid; and what advisory role the Ministry of Defense may have.

To derive an estimate of total FAGIA, we conducted a detailed LexisNexis search of keyword references to China's assistance programs for 2001 to 2011 and made secondary use of data from Congressional Research Service and other sources. Altogether, we obtained 1,055 articles for the ninety-three countries in our study.

Our findings show that the scale of these programs is very large—many times larger than the separate grant-aid development-assistance programs conducted by the United States, Europe, Japan, and other donor countries (Figure 4.1). Newly pledged aid from China was $124.8 billion in 2009, $168.6 billion in 2010, and $189.3 billion in 2011—all far above the $1.7 billion it pledged in 2001. The 2010 and 2011 pledged amounts were equivalent to about 3 percent of China's gross domestic product and were more than twice the size of the officially reported budget of China's Ministry of Defense. This scaling may be misleading because China's FAGIA programs, unlike defense expenditures, are financed by subsidized loans and expected paybacks from them. By way of further comparison, we note that development assistance provided by the US Agency for International Development was $8 billion in 2011 (excluding aid to Iraq and Afghanistan) and that the US Export-Import Bank provided $6.3 billion in worldwide

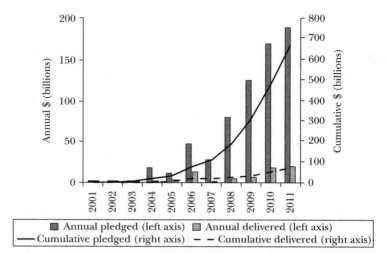

Figure 4.1   China's worldwide annual and cumulative pledged and delivered
FAGIA
Source: Based on data from LexisNexis keyword search.

foreign loans in 2011—although, again, we note that China's programs are more broadly defined than most foreign aid programs.
Whereas most US foreign aid is provided by grants, China's programs are financed by loans. In consequence, and since we do not
know the precise level of subsidization in Chinese official aid and
investment, we cannot directly compare Chinese and Western aid
figures.

There are two principal explanations for these sharp increases.
First, since the 1990s, China has sustained large current account
surpluses, between $200 billion and $350 billion annually, increasing its foreign exchange holdings to more than $1.5 trillion and
providing ample financing for expanding both its aid and its
foreign investments. Second, China's interest in expanding its
foreign sources and supplies of natural resources as a way of sustaining its rapid economic growth has soared.

Actual deliveries of aid lag far behind pledges of assistance;
by our estimate, China has delivered only 9.4 percent of the

FAGIA it has pledged. This is not surprising: Most of these projects may require five years or more to complete. Indeed, we found that pledges roughly match deliveries made six years later. Furthermore, the annual rate of newly pledged assistance has increased sharply in recent years, increasing the gap (and possible time delay) between aid pledges and deliveries.

FAGIA Purposes

Worldwide, natural resource development projects were the purpose of 42 percent of pledged FAGIA funds. Infrastructure projects were the purpose of 40 percent, and other projects, including debt forgiveness and humanitarian aid, made up 18 percent. Infrastructure and natural resource projects often complement each other; roadway access, for example, may be essential for natural resource projects. The programs' amounts and purposes also vary by region.

- Latin America received more aid than any other region between 2001 and 2011. Much of this was for a multicountry natural resource program that included projects in Argentina, Ecuador, Brazil, Chile, and Venezuela. Before 2005, many of the regional programs focused on infrastructure, including power plants, transportation projects, and housing and telecommunications development. China also offered other assistance to two nations in the region that established diplomatic relations with it in the past decade.
- Africa came in second in terms of aid received. Prior to 2004, many of the programs focused on other forms, such as debt cancellation and humanitarian aid. But since then, and especially following China-Africa summits in 2003 and 2006, assistance shifted to a mix of natural resource programs and, especially, infrastructure—including

hydropower, road, and railway projects across Africa. As
part of China's diplomatic efforts, the programs have also
included construction of stadiums and parliamentary build-
ings. Oil was the purpose of most natural resource development programs in Africa, but other projects have sought to
develop resources of gold, platinum, diamonds, uranium,
and aluminum.

- Middle East countries have received aid for oil and gas
  projects, construction of a railway, and debt forgiveness.
  Most large projects in this region aligned with China's
  global resource strategy, to search and explore for oil in
  the Middle East. Most of the other forms of assistance have
  gone to debt forgiveness or cancellation, especially for Iraq.

- FAGIA in South Asia have been unique in focusing on infrastructure and financial aid rather than natural resource
  development. There have been two major initiatives: an economic development package signed in 2006 that includes
  building a seaport, oil refineries, and agricultural advancement, and a $15 billion agreement signed in 2010 for
  constructing two hydropower projects. Pakistan has received
  the overwhelming share of assistance in South Asia, to the
  tune of $89 billion.

- Central Asia received relatively little aid. Most assistance in
  the region was offered to fund oil, natural gas, and mining
  projects. In recent years, regional cooperation organizations such as the Shanghai Cooperation Organisation have
  played a major role in increasing China's multilateral trade
  with the region. This has resulted in several major program
  agreements for regional infrastructure and natural resource
  development.

- FAGIA programs in East Asia reflected a more balanced
  approach than those in other regions (and do not, as we
  consider it, include in-kind assistance to North Korea).

Among North Asian nations, economic development dominated the programs prior to 2006, but infrastructure has since taken over the top spot. Among Southeast Asian nations, infrastructure has accounted for most assistance all along, with the remaining funds focusing on a mix of natural resource and other FAGIA projects. Programs in this region appear to be largely driven by recipient needs, with some exceptions that complement China's interests.

Future Directions

Whether the scale of China's FAGIA will increase, decrease, or remain the same in coming years is unclear. Facing slower economic growth, some policy makers may seek to maintain or even increase the programs as a valuable stimulus for exports. Furthermore, if China's domestic supplies of fossil fuels and key minerals continue to be depleted while industrial demands for them continue to grow, the nation may have incentives to expand its supplies through FAGIA agreements with developing countries and regions. At the same time, competing claimants on domestic, government-financed resources may view reductions of aid as a way to free resources. The People's Liberation Army is one such claimant; others are State Council members concerned with the severe income disparities between the rich, dynamic eastern provinces and the poorer, slower-growing central and western ones. Regardless of future decisions, the pledges China has already made indicate that aid deliveries will remain quite large for at least the next several years.

Note

1. Thomas Lum, "China's Assistance and Government-Sponsored Investment Activities in Africa, Latin America, and Southeast Asia," Congressional Research Service report, 2009.

POSTAUDIT

This RAND study from 2011–2013 highlights the distinctive quid pro quo character of China's foreign assistance. Estimates of China's global assistance are inexact but the best from publicly available data. More accurate numbers probably will be slightly lower than forecasted. *Score: Good*

5   The Strategy behind China's Aid Expansion

In 2001, China spent roughly $1.7 billion on foreign aid. By 2011, the annual foreign aid figure had risen to pledged aid of $189.3 billion. Part of the increase reflects the growth in China's economy. But this is an increase with a purpose, and China's foreign aid programs are as different from aid programs conducted by the United States and other Organisation for Economic Co-operation and Development (OECD) countries as East is from West.

Beijing's aid is explicitly linked to benefits for China as much as it is to benefits for recipients. The aid is financed by loans, while the United States and the OECD subscribe to a definition of "development aid" that confines the term solely to grants. Notably, the quid pro quo aspects of China's aid have a more capitalistic tinge than aid emanating from the capitalist donors, which may be why China's minister of commerce rather than its foreign affairs minister is principally responsible for overseeing the multiple other agencies involved in the programs.

A two-year RAND Corporation study, published in September, by Xiao Wang, Eric Warner, and me, "China's Foreign Aid and Government-Sponsored Investment Activities," documents the

This article was previously published as Charles Wolf Jr., "The Strategy Behind China's Aid Expansion," *Wall Street Journal,* October 8, 2013.

massive size of China's foreign aid programs. Between 2001 and 2011, China's pledged foreign aid was $671 billion, divided among ninety-three emerging-market countries. In 2010, annual aid pledged by China was $169 billion and in 2011, $189 billion—equivalent to about 3 percent of its reported gross domestic product (GDP) and more than twice the size of the officially reported budget of the Ministry of Defense.

Slightly over 80 percent of the pledged aid is allocated for development of natural resources and, secondarily, for infrastructure. The tangible benefits for China are through the explicit consignment of production from the resource development projects for export to China, as specified in the loan agreements that govern the programs. Proceeds from these exports are deposited in escrow accounts established by the two banks that principally fund the programs—the China Development Bank and the Export-Import Bank of China. The loans provided by the banks typically carry 3 percent interest, with repayments scheduled over fifteen years plus a five-year grace period.

China's programs have been under way in all the emerging-market regions. Those receiving the largest amounts are Latin America and Africa, with lesser amounts in the Middle East and Southeast Asia. In Latin America, the largest programs are in Venezuela, Brazil, and Argentina; in Africa, the largest programs are in Nigeria and Ghana; and in Asia, the largest are in Indonesia, Thailand, and Malaysia.

In all regions and countries, China's assistance focuses on the development of natural resources, principally energy related (coal, oil, and gas), and secondarily on ferrous and nonferrous metals. (China's substantial food and fuel aid to North Korea is separate from these programs.)

Both parties presumably benefit from China's aid. Recipients get the stimulus to their economic growth, improved infrastructure, and perhaps exposure to new technology that may be imparted by the programs. China gets an expanded supply of resource commodities expected as payback, which contributes to China's own growth or at least helps avoid further slowdown.

But both parties are also exposed to added risks and hidden costs. The recipient countries experience environmental damage from aggressive Chinese mining and related operations. The thousands of workers imported from China to work on the aid projects create tension and conflict—as shown in press reports from Kenya, Somalia, and other recipient countries—and perhaps lead to increased corruption within recipient countries.

Although there's a risk that the vulnerable financial circumstances of some borrowers may delay repayments or otherwise result in nonperformance, China may make agreements to avoid defaults. Financially pressed borrowers will be asked for concessions or accommodations such as according favorable access to Chinese investors or granting wider scope for the number and activities of China's "soft-power" Confucian Institutes that expand awareness and understanding of China's culture and language. Other concessions linked to debt forgiveness or extended or refinanced loans may involve the granting of port-of-call and refueling rights for People's Liberation Army naval vessels or landing rights for PLA air units.

There are reasons to believe that China's recently expanded foreign aid programs will continue. For example, maintaining or even increasing aid may provide a stimulus to exports and so are welcomed as a partial offset to the slowdown in China's GDP growth.

Arguing for a reduction in aid are the already-tightened budget constraints and competing claims inside China. From the northern and western provinces, for instance, come demands for clean water supplies. Nationwide, there is a compelling need to address health and other hazards of atmospheric pollution and intensified urbanization—and the large volume of public and private debt throughout the economy. China also faces the growing burden of an aging population and the mounting costs of military modernization. The greater the costs of China's foreign aid, the tighter the constraints facing these claimants.

Recognizing that the complexity and the opacity of China's decision making make predictions difficult, it still seems likely that China will continue as a major participant in the aid business—although at a somewhat reduced level, perhaps with lower subsidies and more-collateralized borrowing. No less and perhaps even more than what the United States has experienced in six decades of foreign aid, China's large ventures in this realm will encounter unintended and perverse consequences. China is as likely to regret as to savor the experience.

POSTAUDIT

This distillation of a prior RAND study (summarized in Chapter 4) provides a new forecast of future Chinese foreign assistance. The interval since the article was written in 2013 is too short to accord much prescience to forecast. *Score: Good*

---

6 A Truly Great Leap Forward

Ronald Coase ranks among the world's most influential economists, yet he rarely appears in the media spotlight. That's because he channels his influence through other economists while maintaining a prudent distance from the glare of quotidian policy disputes. Coase, who received the Nobel Prize in Economics in 1991, has originated some of the most important economic ideas of recent years. These include the eponymous Coase theorem, which states that strong, precisely defined property rights can reduce the social costs of private transactions. He also pioneered the law-and-economics field, using economic insights to illuminate legal problems. He's 102, yet his intellectual output remains dazzling.

In *How China Became Capitalist*, Coase and Ning Wang, an assistant professor of global studies at Arizona State University, offer a "historical narrative of the chain of actions" that brought about China's remarkable transformation from a deeply impoverished socialist country to the world's second-largest economy.

Yet to describe the book simply as "historical narrative" would be a misstatement. Messrs. Coase and Wang interpret China's rise

This article was previously published as Charles Wolf Jr., "A Truly Great Leap Forward," *Wall Street Journal*, April 30, 2013, http://online.wsj.com/articles/SB10001424127887323335404578444792065046344.

in terms that are distinctly different from what has been accepted as conventional wisdom, which holds that China's dramatic rise has resulted from astute guidance by its Communist Party leadership. But as the authors demonstrate, China's dramatic economic growth over the past three decades hasn't been a top-down process engineered by party leaders in Beijing. Instead, China's rise has been a bottom-up process driven by what the authors call the "four marginal revolutions."

First came the "household responsibility system" in agriculture that, the authors say, "emerged spontaneously in rural China" in the late 1970s and was implemented nationwide in 1982. This system allowed farmers to sell some of their output at free-market prices. The next revolution resulted from rural industry reform in the form of township and village enterprises, which impelled townships to behave as entrepreneurs in producing and marketing their products. These enterprises in turn led to the emergence of entrepreneurs and the "individual economy"—"a euphemism for private economy," the authors explain, that was intended to disguise the underlying capitalist reality of this third revolution. The fourth revolution was the establishment of the "special economic zones" in Shenzhen and several other towns in Guangdong and Fujian provinces and in Shanghai and other coastal cities.

According to the authors, the four marginal revolutions gave birth to "a vibrant non-state sector" that contrasted sharply with "a stagnant state sector." These developments followed the Great Leap Forward in the late 1950s—when millions starved as a result of misguided collectivization and industrialization efforts—and the Cultural Revolution in the mid-1960s, "Mao's last and most horrendous effort to mold China into socialism," as the authors put it.

Viewed against the backdrop of these catastrophes, the achievements of this private sector activity were extraordinary and sometimes bizarre. By the early 1980s, the authors write, "self-employed barbers came to earn higher incomes than surgeons in state hospitals. Street vendors . . . earned more than nuclear scientists. Traders, small-shop and private restaurant owners . . . were among the highest income groups in China." And "the number of self-employed household businesses and single proprietorships increased from 140,000 in 1978 to 2.6 million in 1981."

The Communist Party's role in bringing this to pass, the authors say, consisted mainly in getting out of the way. Messrs. Coase and Wang conclude that "the gradual withdrawal of government from the economy, rather than the strength or omnipresence of the political leadership . . . explains the success." The guiding principles have been pragmatism, experimentation, and the Confucian injunction "to seek truth from facts"—or, as Deng Xiaoping, who pushed through many of the post-Mao reforms, put it in a famous dictum, "Practice is the sole criterion for testing truth."

How China Became Capitalist abounds with such insights. For example, the authors distinguish between, on one hand, rule *by* law governing hierarchical relations and, on the other, rule *of* law governing horizontal relations. Rule by law is plainly manifest in China, in how severe punishment is applied in some instances of corruption (while others are ignored). But rule of law is rarely evident: the Communist Party brutally suppresses political dissent as well as expressions of individual or group identity that might threaten its rule. Messrs. Coase and Wang deplore China's lack of a "free market for ideas" and the damage that this has wrought on universities and on the Chinese economy's capacity to innovate.

The authors also insist that the future dynamism of China's economy depends on the continued growth of its private sector. But they are much less clear on the future of China's huge state-owned enterprises and of China's partial efforts to privatize them.

Occasionally the authors' contentions are problematic. For example, they opine that a free market for ideas can be sustained without political democracy. Actually, it's hard to imagine one without the other: Some of the ideas on offer, after all, might strongly advocate expanded democracy, which is anathema to China's leaders. And although the authors acknowledge the centrality of property rights in effective market reform, they avoid the question of whether property rights, if not regulated, may sometimes be exercised at the expense of human rights.

And while *How China Became Capitalist* is tightly written and swept relatively clear of excessive economic jargon, it isn't easy reading. The book is crammed with facts, data, cross-references, and twenty-one pages of carefully crafted endnotes. Yet patient readers will be rewarded with a better and deeper understanding of the most extraordinary transformation in modern economic history.

POSTAUDIT

Ronald Coase's demise since the publication of his book was not foreseen in my review. However, the review's testimonial to the book's merit and its author's acuity remains valid. The book is likely to be a classic in the field. *Score: Good*

7   A Smarter Approach to the Yuan

The best law schools and public policy graduate schools inculcate in their students an ability to make the strongest possible case in favor of a position or policy with which they disagree. The test of whether the lesson has been truly learned is whether those who favor the position would accept its rendition as a fair and effective representation of why they favor it.

With this in mind, I present the argument for the US stance favoring a substantial rise in the undervalued Chinese yuan. The US position has been repeatedly stated, albeit in abbreviated and nuanced form, by President Barack Obama and Treasury Secretary Timothy Geithner. It is also reflected in the large bipartisan majority in the House of Representatives that approved legislation to allow a retaliatory tariff on China's exports to the United States unless China revalues its currency. It has been expressed more vociferously and combatively by key leaders in the Senate, and by politically charged commentators, including Paul Krugman.

This article was previously published as Charles Wolf Jr., "A Smarter Approach to the Yuan," *Policy Review*, April 1, 2011, http://www.hoover.org/research /smarter-approach-yuan.

Once the case for this pro position has been presented fairly
and fully, I explain why I think it is fundamentally wrong. I then go
on to suggest measures that would be more appropriate and effective in contributing to a "rebalancing" of China's international
accounts as well as those of the United States than would a revaluation of the Chinese yuan.

In early January, when President Hu Jintao met in Washington,
DC, with President Obama, the agenda for the meeting deftly
acknowledged the presidents' disagreement on the currency issue
without discussing, let alone resolving, it.

The Case for Revaluing the Yuan

The Chinese yuan (also known as the renminbi, or "people's currency") trades in foreign exchange markets at a rate of approximately 6.7 yuan per dollar (equivalent to about fifteen US cents
per yuan). Another measure that accords the yuan a considerably higher value is based on the goods and services the yuan can
buy within China compared to what these same goods and services would cost in the United States. This rate is referred to as
the yuan's purchasing power parity (PPP). The PPP valuation of
the yuan is roughly two or three times higher (between 2.2 and
3.4 yuan per US dollar, or between thirty and forty US cents per
yuan) than the market exchange rate.

Associated with the yuan's value in foreign exchange markets
is the fact that the value of China's global exports of goods and
services perennially exceeds by large amounts the value of its
imports. Indeed, this excess has often been larger than the combined trade surpluses of the two countries that have the world's
next-largest trade surpluses, Germany and Japan. China's annual
global trade surplus is currently about $200 billion; the surplus
has been considerably larger in prior years. More than half this

global surplus is China's bilateral trade surplus with the United States. When China's net current earnings from other sources besides trade—including its net receipts from accumulated prior Chinese investments in the United States, Europe, Asia, and the rest of the world and the remittances it receives from Chinese residents abroad—are added to its trade surplus, the result is a Chinese global current account surplus amounting to about $300 billion annually.

The value of a currency that underpins such a large surplus would normally be expected to rise (that is, to appreciate). The reason for this expected revaluation is that the dollar demand for that currency (the yuan) by other countries to pay for the imports they receive from China greatly exceeds the supply of yuan resulting from China's requirements to pay for the imports it receives from the United States and the rest of the world.

But this normal revaluation process is thwarted because China interferes with the functioning of this standard demand-supply interaction. China does this by withdrawing the surplus dollars from the exchange market, thus neutralizing their effects on the exchange value of the yuan. This is accomplished by compensating exporters for their dollar earnings through direct issuance to them of additional domestic yuan and then sterilizing the additional yuan by selling government bonds to absorb the expanded supply of yuan currency. This tidy result removes the surplus dollars from foreign exchange markets while also limiting, if not eliminating, the risk of domestic inflation that might otherwise ensue because of the increased currency generated by exports and circulating in domestic Chinese markets.

China is thus said to be guilty of manipulating the yuan's value by preventing its appreciation and keeping it below its equilibrium value. Such manipulation implicitly subsidizes China's exports, because the dollar cost of its exports is less than would be the case if the yuan were allowed to appreciate. The lower dollar cost of its exports thus enables China to maintain its trade and its current account surpluses, impeding the ability of other countries to expand their exports and to gain momentum for what in many instances—notably in the United States and much of Western Europe—has been a distinctly mild recovery from the Great Recession.

Therefore, it is argued that China can and should appreciate its currency—that is, revalue the yuan upward. The yuan should appreciate to a rate of, say, five yuan per dollar (twenty US cents per yuan, rather than the current value of fifteen cents), thereby making China's exports more expensive—hence, tending to decrease them. At the same time, this revaluation would make China's imports from the United States and the rest of the world less expensive, because fewer of the higher-valued yuan would be needed to buy dollar imports, which would tend to increase as a result.

The argument concludes that, in the interest of both bilateral and global rebalancing, China should be persuaded or pressured to move in this direction. The official US position urges persuasion; the more combative stance of prominent US lawmakers and pundits favors pressure.

The Case against Revaluation

The answer requires looking at the Chinese economy from the inside out rather than from the outside in, which is the more usual perspective adopted by the revaluation advocates.

What is striking about this inward look is that it highlights the extraordinarily high level of China's domestic savings: between 45 and 50 percent of gross domestic product (GDP)! Such a high savings rate is without precedent during peacetime in modern economic history and is particularly rare in emerging-market economies. It also flies in the face of conventional development theory. The theory presumes that, because developing countries are poor, they will have to consume most of what they produce and to invest the remainder. As a result, so the theory goes, developing countries will have low savings rates, as well as trade deficits rather than surpluses, and therefore will need financial transfers and inward-bound investment from wealthier developed countries to supplement the developing countries' low savings and to pay for their trade deficits.

China stands as a striking counterexample to this standard model because it has an amazingly high savings rate (three or four times that of most developed countries, including the United States), accompanied by a large and growing volume of outward-bound foreign investment.

China has an amazingly high savings rate—three or four times that of most developed countries, including the United States. China's high savings rate—comprising the combined savings of privately owned and state-owned companies, households, township and village enterprises, cooperatives, and central and local government—is hard to explain. Despite the extensive research under way within and outside China, an adequate explanation is still elusive. The reason for its elusiveness probably lies in the numerous contributing factors that vary in their prior, current, and future influence on savings behavior by households, individuals, companies, and central and provincial governments.

Demography figures prominently among the contributing factors. China's population is aging rapidly: The proportion of its elderly (over age sixty-five) will nearly double in the next fifteen years. China's dependency ratio (dependents as percentage of those of working age) will rise by nearly 50 percent within this period, and most of this increase will be due to the increasing numbers of elderly, their expectation of higher health care costs in the future, and their hope to ease the burden of these future costs by accumulating current savings.

China's long-standing one-child family policy has been a significant contributor to these trends, reducing the potential sources of support for aging parents and hence increasing the latter's savings propensity. Another demographic imponderable that may affect savings behavior is the marked gender imbalance among China's younger-age cohorts—between 15 percent and 30 percent more males than females across China's thirty-seven provinces and special administrative regions. Fear by elder family members that a single male offspring might emigrate in the absence of a suitable marital partner in China may also conduce to precautionary savings.

Along with these demographic trends, increased savings throughout Chinese society and social structure have doubtless been galvanized by delayed development of an adequate social security safety net. What has been taking shape in China is a social security system whose components will include a part that is based on defined contributions by the covered populace and a part that is a specified floor of defined benefits underwritten by the state. Although system development is under way, the delay has doubtless stimulated higher savings rates as a source of protection for and by China's rapidly aging population.

But more than demography and social security affect savings in China. The rapid pace of economic growth and the rise in wages and other income that their recipients haven't yet adjusted to may be another part of the explanation. Finally, the prevalence in some circles of generally bearish uncertainties about whether China will be able to sustain its rapid growth may be a further contributor to abnormally high savings as a form of protection against a possible future downturn.

China's annual global trade surplus of about $200 billion reflects the excess of its savings above its investment. Whatever the validity and differing weight accorded to these numerous factors, China's huge savings rate exceeds its investment rate by 6–7 percent of GDP. This excess is crucial for understanding China's trade surpluses and current account surpluses. The excess is also central to consideration of what might be done about China's excess savings that would reduce these surpluses, whereas tinkering with its exchange rate would not.

Central to this understanding is an inexorable economic relationship: namely, the excess of any country's domestic savings above its domestic investment must be exactly equal to the excess of its exports of goods and services above its imports of goods and services. In other words, its savings surplus must equal its trade surplus! The relationship is inexorable because it follows from the way that the component elements are defined.

The intuitive common sense behind the relationship can be grasped by thinking of the trade surplus as a bundle of goods and services. That this bundle is saved means it is neither consumed nor invested domestically. The trade (savings) surplus can't be an addition to domestic inventories because additions to inventories constitute investment, whereas the bundle represents the excess of savings above investment. Instead, the surplus bundle, as a part of China's GDP, flows abroad to global markets. The savings surplus and the trade surplus are identical!

China's annual global trade surplus of about $200 billion reflects the excess of its savings (45 to 50 percent of GDP) above its investment (about 40 percent of GDP). The current account surplus consists of this trade surplus plus its other net current international receipts. As I noted earlier, these current international receipts consist principally of earnings from China's accumulated and continuing investments abroad, including about $40 billion in payments by the US Treasury to service China's holdings of more than $1.6 trillion of US government securities. China's nontrade receipts also include earnings from its other holdings of about $800 billion of additional foreign assets—both corporate assets and sovereign debt assets—and remittances by Chinese residents abroad to recipients in China.

To count as add-ons to its current account surpluses, China's current earnings from accumulated assets must be net of the earnings acquired by foreign investments in China. However, because China's corporate and other income taxes are generally lower than corresponding taxes levied in the United States and in Europe, foreign investors in China often prefer to meet their tax liabilities in China, to retain their after-tax earnings in the form of yuan holdings, and thus to forgo seeking to convert and remit them as dollars or euros to their homelands. So the proportion and amounts of China's earnings from its investments that are remitted to China and hence add to its current account surpluses tend to be larger than the proportion and amounts of earnings by foreign investors in China that these investors remit to their own countries. It is an interesting facet of China's own non-trade earnings that, by adding to its current account surplus, they indirectly contribute financing for subsequent additional cross-border investments by state-owned and nonstate enterprises in buying foreign companies or equities in these companies, thereby generating additional earnings in the future.

Revaluation would likely be followed by keen disappointment among its advocates and their sharp recriminations. What I have referred to as an inexorable relationship underlying China's trade surpluses is an iron law—what economists refer to as an "identity," which simply means that the components of GDP—investment, consumption, and imports and exports—are so defined that the numbers measuring them must conform to this identity. The identity doesn't say anything about causation—about the many influences that affect the size of savings, consumption, investment, and imports and exports—but it does establish inexorably how the parts relate to each other.

China's savings surplus is equal to China's trade surplus. Hence, as long as the surplus of China's domestic savings over its domestic investment persists, tinkering with the pegged exchange rate will have only slight and transitory effects on China's imports and exports. Changing the yuan-dollar peg from fifteen cents per yuan to twenty cents would soon be offset by a compensating fall in China's export prices and a compensating rise in its import prices. This sequence of events would ensue as a result of the inexorable identity between the savings surplus and the trade surplus.

There is another reason why the offsetting price adjustments would be quick and decisive. Much of China's exports consist of value added to imported inputs by processing imported raw materials and intermediate products to produce the final products for export. For example, imports of iron ore, copper, aluminum, cotton, and wool are processed and fabricated, subsequently emerging as exports of consumer products and machinery; and imports of computer chips and hard drives subsequently result in China's exports of electronic and computer products. Often the value added by processing and finishing in China is less than half the corresponding final export from China. Were the yuan to be revalued, the nearly immediate consequence would be to lower the prices of imported inputs sufficiently to compensate, and in many instances to overcompensate, for what might otherwise be reflected in higher prices of the exported final products.

Finally, because of the negligible effects that revaluation would have on China's global surplus and on its bilateral surplus with the United States, if revaluation were nonetheless to occur, it would probably have distinctly adverse political repercussions, quite apart from the absent economic effects. Revaluation would likely be followed by keen disappointment among its advocates and their sharp recriminations. Failure to realize the hoped-for turnaround in the bilateral trade balance would be attributed to various barriers impeding American exporters' access to China's domestic markets. Various types of nontrade barriers already and often afford preferential treatment to China's own domestic firms relative to foreign firms in China. But the consequence of a failure of revaluation to achieve the results sought by its advocates would likely be a freshet of hostile charges and countercharges with adverse effects on US-China relations.

A Better Way?

For the trade (savings) surplus to diminish and a significant rebalancing to occur, China should increase domestic consumption (decrease savings) more directly, more rapidly, and by larger amounts than it has done so far.

This can be done through various measures. For example, taxes can be levied on savings above specified savings thresholds. In the tax filings of urban nonstate and state-owned enterprises and of urban households and individuals, a savings threshold above, say, 30 percent of income after allowing for recorded investment expenditures by businesses and consumption expenditures by households could be subject to heavy taxation. Excessive saving above this threshold would thereby be discouraged. Moreover, the revenues produced by the tax levy could help finance accelerated development of the planned social security safety net referred to earlier.

Additionally, excessive saving can be discouraged and added consumption can be encouraged by active yet prudent expansion of consumer credit.

I make this suggestion in full recognition that, if an American economist proposes the idea, it is likely—and with good reason—to be viewed by China's bankers and policy makers as ironic and hubristic. After all, one of the two or three principal causes of the global financial crisis was the egregious and imprudent expansion of consumer credit in the United States preceding the Great Recession of 2008 and 2009. Subprime and Alt-A mortgages extended in huge volumes to credit-unworthy borrowers by US lending institutions, and then irresponsibly guaranteed with the "full faith and credit of the United States government" by Fannie Mae and Freddie Mac, were the largest and most flagrant part of the consumer credit bubble flooding the American economy in the first decade of the twenty-first century. So in advancing the suggestion to rapidly expand consumer credit in China, I feel obliged to accompany it with an ample dose of humility.

Nevertheless, there is a big difference between what was an imprudently excessive volume of consumer credit in the United States in the years preceding the Great Recession and the presently constricted availability of consumer credit in China. For example, the ratio of consumer credit to GDP in China is currently 17 percent, compared with 40 percent in South Korea, 54 percent in Taiwan, and 65 percent in Malaysia. Furthermore, availability of consumer credit cards and debit cards is much more limited in China than in the other emerging-market countries in its neighborhood. Thus, there is ample room for China to combine prudence with stimulus in encouraging consumption and curtailing excessive saving. Regulating the expansion of consumer credit, and preventing its abuse, can be readily accomplished in China by extending the purview of China's Banking Regulatory Commission. There would be no need to embark on anything like the Dodd-Frank financial regulatory legislation in the United States, which, within its two-thousand-plus pages, created the Consumer Financial Protection Bureau to guard against abuse of the various forms of consumer credit extensions.

There has been a misplaced focus in the soi-disant currency wars on the central importance of the yuan's peg to the dollar. By targeting the repositories and sources of excessive savings, the measures I've described would affect the basic relationship underlying China's trade (i.e., savings) surplus and its current account surplus, whereas exchange-rate tinkering will not. By reducing the excess of its savings over its investments, these measures will decrease China's global trade surplus, as well as its current account surplus, and thereby contribute to global rebalancing.

In furtherance of some degree of global rebalancing, there has been a misplaced focus in the soi-disant currency wars on the central importance of the yuan's peg to the dollar. In reality, this mistaken focus will have little if any effect on global imbalances, and such effects as it may have will at most be transitory for the many reasons I've discussed. Instead, the focus of rebalancing efforts and debate should be on the real underlying problem—namely, China's excessive savings.

In the longer-term future, issues connected with valuation of the yuan might be resolved if China were to move to floating its currency and allowing a freely functioning foreign exchange market to determine the yuan's changing market value. China's previous prime minister, Zhu Rongji, endorsed this prospect several years ago to take place in an indefinitely distant future. Of course, such a scenario is precluded in the nearer term by the limited convertibility of the yuan for capital transactions.

In any event, those who may favor this prospect, including me, should bear in mind that, if it were to occur in something earlier than a very distant future, the yuan would be as likely to depreciate as to appreciate! At present, China's banks have on their balance sheets more than 70 trillion yuan (about $10 trillion) in liquid deposits held by companies, households, individuals, cooperatives, and other entities—a sum that is twice the size of China's GDP. Were full convertibility to be realized, some of the holders of these yuan assets would doubtless seek diversification of their holdings by converting a part of them to nonyuan assets, including dollar and euro assets. With the resulting increased demand by yuan-asset holders for nondollar assets, the yuan's value would likely decline.

This scenario seems remote at present but, with changing circumstances, its remote future may become a more plausible present.

Where Does This Leave Us?

The preceding discussion appears to place all the burden of global rebalancing on China. In fact, the burden should be shared by the United States, which should undertake precisely the opposite measures as China. Such reciprocal measures are necessary to reduce the chronic global trade and current account deficits of the United States by reducing the shortfall of its domestic savings compared to its aggregate investments. The excess of China's savings above its investment, which most of the preceding discussion has emphasized, is distressingly paralleled by a shortfall of US savings below its own investments.

This shortfall includes the savings and investments of both federal and state governments—mostly large negative savings by these governments in recent years—and of US companies, individuals, households, and other entities. Together, these result in a recurring shortfall in US savings of about 3 to 4 percent of the US GDP, largely made up of substantial dissavings (negative savings, thus requiring borrowing) by government and only modestly positive savings by households and retained corporate earnings in the rest of the economy.

While the burden of global rebalancing should impinge on the United States as well as China, there is a critical asymmetry in the respective burdens they can bear. Measures required in China to reduce savings and boost consumption affect a Chinese economy that is buoyed by a real rate of GDP growth that remains high—above 9 percent. In sharp contrast, the measures required by the United States to limit consumption and raise savings would, in the short run, depress an already low rate of growth and an anemic recovery from the Great Recession accompanied by a near 10 percent rate of unemployment.

As a consequence of these immediate problems—problems that are made more serious because of political rather than economic considerations—US monetary and fiscal policy makers have been more concerned with trying to boost the economic recovery by encouraging domestic consumption and investment rather than addressing the underlying imbalance of a deficiency of aggregate savings compared to relatively excessive consumption and investment—the precise opposite of China's imbalance. The Federal Reserve's announcement at the end of 2010 of its second so-called quantitative easing (QE2) illustrates the short-term priorities of monetary policy in the United States.

China should be more able to rein in savings and increase consumption than the United States to cut consumption and boost savings. QE2 consists of a $600 billion fund intended to monetize public debt, boost the money supply, and flatten the yield curve on government bonds by lowering longer-term yields. The goals of QE2 are to promote investment and job growth through lower interest rates on corporate and other fixed-income securities. The goals and the measures to advance them are understandable for the short-term reasons mentioned above. However, these measures run in a direction opposite to what is required for a better degree of long-term rebalancing of the US international accounts. To further the longer-term rebalancing objective, US policy should seek to raise aggregate savings above aggregate investment: more specifically, to tamp down consumption, both private and public, reflected in smaller budgets and lower deficits in the budgets of federal and state governments. These are essential goals in the longer term, while the time horizons of political actors tend to be more or less coincident with the shorter terms for which they are elected and in which they usually aspire to be reelected.

As a consequence, in the short run, the relatively heavier lifting to advance global rebalancing can more plausibly be borne by China because its efforts to sustain high GDP growth have been successful, whereas US efforts to resume ample growth have been much less so.

What this means in practical terms is that China should be more able to rein in savings and increase consumption than the United States will be able to curtail consumption and increase savings. From China's point of view, reluctance to shoulder this heavier burden arises from the risk it entails of adding to the inflationary pressures recently evident in the Chinese economy. Current inflation in China has more than quadrupled over its rate not long ago: between 4 and 5 percent currently versus approximately stable prices in 2009. Efforts to boost consumption by the sorts of measures discussed earlier would likely add to the inflationary risks. Still, by combining a rise in prime interest rates (currently between 3 and 4 percent) with a rise in reserve requirements for its banks (recently raised to 19.5 percent), along with appropriate administrative measures, China's policy makers should be able to navigate these moderately roiling waters.

According to a familiar scriptural precept (Luke 12:48), "To whom much is given, from him much will be required; and to whom much has been committed, of him they will ask the more." Similar advice to a wise governor is provided by Confucius (*Analects*, chapter 12, section 2): "Wishing to be established himself, he assists others to be established; wishing to be successful himself, he assists others to be successful.

POSTAUDIT

Whether China's currency (alternately referred to as yuan
or renminbi) is undervalued or overvalued, why this should
be so, and what to do about it remains controversial—in the
United States, in China, and in global financial circles. My
judgment is that, under conditions of full rather than partial convertibility, the yuan is more likely to depreciate than
appreciate. The analysis in this article (written in 2011) presents both sides of the controversy and the reasons for my
conclusion. *Score: Good*

8   Our Misplaced Yuan Worries

It's conventional wisdom that bipartisanship results in improved public policy. That this is not so is strikingly illustrated by a bill, supported by Democratic chairmen and ranking Republican members of the relevant committees in the Senate and House, that would punish China for its "misaligned" currency (the yuan). Its mistaken premise is that this misalignment threatens our prosperity by causing America's large current account deficits with China.

In 2007, China's current account surplus—the sum of its trade surplus and net receipts from foreign assets and foreign remittances—will be nearly 10 percent of its gross domestic product (GDP), or about $300 billion. Two-thirds of this represents a bilateral surplus with the United States. The US global current account deficit in 2007 will be about $800 billion, nearly 6 percent of the US GDP. Thus, China's bilateral current account surplus with the United States is one-quarter of the global US deficit.

In 2005, the yuan was worth 12 US cents. It is currently worth 13.5 cents. Many believe that if the yuan's exchange value were

This article was previously published as Charles Wolf Jr., "Our Misplaced Yuan Worries," *Wall Street Journal,* December 15, 2007, http://www.hoover.org /research/our-misplaced-yuan-worries.

to increase further, perhaps to 17 cents or 18 cents, the bilateral imbalance between the two countries would be substantially reduced, if not eliminated. China's exports to the United States would thereby become more expensive in US dollars and would therefore decrease, while China's imports from the United States would become less expensive in Chinese yuan and therefore would increase. If China fails to make this currency adjustment, the pending legislation in Congress would impose a tax on imports from China to offset the putative currency undervaluation.

This reasoning, though plausible, is wrong. A country's global current account deficit depends on the excess of its gross domestic investment over gross domestic savings. Gross savings in the United States are 10 to 12 percent of GDP, largely consisting of corporate depreciation allowances and retained corporate earnings. On the other hand, gross domestic investment is 16 to 17 percent of GDP. The difference between the two is the US current account deficit.

China's current account surplus is the mirror image of the US imbalance. Gross investment in China is above 30 percent of its GDP, but its savings are even higher, above 40 percent.

While the appreciation of the yuan might initially raise US exports to China and lower China's exports to the United States, these effects would be small and transitory as long as the imbalances between savings and investment in the two economies persist. Japan and Germany—two countries with perennial current account surpluses—illustrate the point.

While Japan's yen has appreciated against the dollar in the past several years, its current account surplus is largely unchanged, because Japan's domestic savings have continued to exceed its domestic investment. The euro has appreciated 30 percent relative to the dollar, yet Germany maintains a large global current account surplus. That's because the German economy maintains an excess of savings over investment. (The economies of most other eurozone countries show a savings shortfall and continue to incur current account deficits.)

In both Germany and Japan, the excess of domestic savings over domestic investment persists and hence their current account surpluses persist, notwithstanding their currencies' appreciation.

To reduce the bilateral imbalances between China and the United States requires more carefully crafted policies than revaluation of the yuan, else the results could be perverse. If correcting China's imbalance were sought by increasing gross domestic investment to match domestic savings, rampant inflation above the present 6.6 percent annual rate (already twice that of a year ago) could result—because soaring demand for materials, plant, and equipment would in the near term sharply boost their prices. This is a sequence China is already experiencing. If correcting the US imbalance were sought by lowering investment to a level closer to the US current savings rate, a serious recession would likely result.

Effective remedial policies for China lie in raising domestic consumption (reducing domestic savings) by 4 or 5 percent of GDP through such measures as wider dissemination of credit and debit cards and other consumer credit instruments. Remedial policies for the United States lie in raising current savings by 2 or 3 percent of US GDP, through curbing government spending, instituting personal retirement accounts to supplement the defined benefits of Social Security, establishing a graduated consumption tax, or a combination of these measures.

In the United States, such measures have been advocated by some members of both parties. But more important than their potential bipartisan support, they would warrant nonpartisan support because, unlike currency realignment, they would actually address the underlying sources of the US and Chinese imbalances.

POSTAUDIT

Written before the Great Recession in 2008, this article
argues that China's allegedly undervalued currency neither
adversely nor significantly affected the US economy—despite
a consensus between Republicans and Democrats that the
reverse is true. Bipartisanship does not imply sensible policy.
Score: Good

9   Chinese Fire Drill

Forget tinkering with the renminbi's dollar peg. The key is to increase consumption.

A strident chorus has lately attacked China's stubborn adherence to its policy of maintaining a narrowly controlled renminbi peg to the US dollar. The chorus includes senior US government officials, politicians turned economists, economists turned political scientists, and political scientists turned financial experts. The choral theme proclaims that appreciation of the renminbi by perhaps 20 percent to 40 percent is essential for good things to happen and bad consequences to be avoided. The narrow band within which China has announced it will allow the peg to fluctuate is said to be drastically insufficient. "It's time to get tough with China," goes the choral refrain.

Most of this flies in the face of basic economics. It also ignores an inevitable question that, although rarely asked, is one whose answer, unlike currency revaluation, could indeed contribute to making things better all around.

The basic economics that the chorus ignores resides in an inexorable accounting identity: the difference between an economy's

This article was previously published as Charles Wolf Jr., "Chinese Fire Drill," *International Economy*, Summer 2010, 34–35.

(in this instance, China's) aggregate domestic savings and its aggregate investment must equal the difference between its international earnings and its international payments (that is, China's current account surplus). Put simply, a country's excess savings are inextricably linked to an equivalent excess of its international earnings from exports and other sources over its international payments for imports and other obligations. China's aggregate savings at about 45 percent of gross domestic product (GDP) exceed aggregate investment by perhaps 10 percent of GDP.

The inevitable question that needs to be asked is why doesn't China's leadership—the Political Bureau of the Standing Committee of the Communist Party, and the State Council of the Chinese government—move aggressively to boost domestic consumption, thereby changing the parameters of the accounting equation, enhancing the government's popular appeal, complying with China's formal commitment to "rebalance" its international accounts, and modestly shrinking China's current account surplus?

Movement in this direction will benefit China and its trading partners (including the United States), while appreciation of the renminbi will not.

Although the call for revaluing the renminbi is misguided, it seems at first glance to make sense. If the renminbi were revalued from ¥6.8 per US dollar to, say, ¥5 per dollar, the renminbi prices of Chinese imports from the United States would initially decline, and China's imports would tend to increase. Similarly, revaluation would initially raise the dollar prices of imports from China, and US imports from China would tend to decrease.

However, as long as the elements in the inexorable accounting identity hold—and therefore China's savings continue to hugely exceed its investments—the tendencies implied by revaluation will be negligible and transitory. Offsets to the revaluation's effects will ensue through quick adjustments of renminbi import prices and of the dollar prices charged to US importers. Renminbi import prices will tend to rise, while the dollar prices charged to US importers will tend to fall because aggregate savings continue to exceed aggregate investment, and earnings from China's international transactions will continue to exceed its international payments.

For appreciable rebalancing to occur, the avoided but inevitable question needs to be asked and resolved: Why don't China's policy makers move aggressively to boost domestic consumption? For example, if the economy's enormous savings ratio of 45 percent of GDP were to be reduced by, say, 7–8 percent (that is, consumption were to rise), the parameters of the accounting identity would be changed; by contrast, currency revaluation would not change them. Moreover, these changes can be accomplished through fiscal and credit policies that, unlike currency revaluation, will have direct and lasting effects, benefiting both China and its trading partners and silencing the voluble critics.

The appropriate policy measures include easing of bank provision of consumer credit, facilitating wider issuance of credit and debit cards, and expediting the expansion of social security support by both the government and corporate providers. The first two measures will directly boost consumption, and the third will indirectly help raise consumption by allaying the widespread precautionary motives that lead to excessively high household and business savings.

If the benefits from such policies are evident, why don't China's policy makers move aggressively to implement them? The question is inevitable, but the answer is elusive. Perhaps the answer lies in the leadership's deeply ingrained political and cultural conservatism. Economic growth and improvements in living standards in China over the past three decades have already been noteworthy. Might still further improvement be too much? Might a still more rapid pace be too fast? If improvements were to accelerate

further, might the public become too self-confident, too demand-
ing? Might this in turn lead to demands for political democracy
and to restiveness at one-party authoritarianism? And might all of
this accelerated change further threaten or abridge the remnant
traditions of Chinese culture and Confucian society?

The inevitable question and its corollaries need to be asked.
Even if answers are elusive, focusing on them is a better bet than
tinkering with the renminbi's dollar peg.

POSTAUDIT

This essay's contention that rebalancing China's economy
requires boosting its domestic consumption—rather than
tinkering with exchange rates—is equally valid in 2014 as
when written in 2010. *Score: Good*

10   A Liberated Yuan Is Likely to Fall

"Currency manipulation" is a charge repeatedly leveled against China in recent years. Prior to 2014, US pundits and lawmakers denounced interventions by its central bank, the People's Bank of China, that prevented the yuan's rise from about sixteen cents (6.25 yuan per US dollar) to what critics construed to be an appropriately higher, market-based value—about twenty cents (5 yuan per dollar). The higher valuation presumably would benefit US exports and US international accounts more generally.

The International Monetary Fund also chimed in last year, saying China's manipulation of the yuan's exchange rate was a distinct possibility. This, the IMF said, would be detrimental to market-based exchange rates and freely operating international trade and investment.

Now critics in the financial media have reversed direction, claiming that the People's Bank of China is contriving to weaken the yuan's value, thereby seeking to promote its exports and stimulate the country's lagging growth.

Yet if the central bank does reflect, or were to reflect, the increased reliance on market forces recently pledged by China's top political leadership (the Third Party Plenum's "Decision

This article was previously published as Charles Wolf Jr., "A Liberated Yuan Is Likely to Fall," *Wall Street Journal,* April 21, 2014, http://on.wsj.com/14XWey7.

Concerning Comprehensively Deepening the Reform," January 16, 2014), the yuan's value is likely to gravitate toward the lower end of the sixteen–twenty cents range or even slightly below it. Three factors will contribute to this outcome.

First, Beijing seeks to make the yuan a major international reserve and invoicing currency, aspiring to share this role with the US dollar or (less likely) to replace it. China's recent proliferation of swap accounts with several of its principal trading partners in Europe and Asia—denominating the accounts in yuan—indicates this aspiration.

Second, to achieve status as a major reserve currency, the yuan must be fully convertible on the capital account. Currently, capital transactions, such as efforts by Alibaba to have its shares listed on the New York Stock Exchange and by Huawei to buy shares of US companies, require that the Chinese companies' yuan capital be readily convertible into US dollars. Such convertibility is easily accessible for China's favored state-owned companies (such as China Petroleum Company [Sinopec] and China National Offshore Oil Corporation) and for some approved private entities (such as Huawei and Alibaba). For others, both corporate and individual, convertibility into dollars or other foreign currencies is restricted.

The third factor is the enormous size of accumulated liquid deposits on the balance sheets of China's financial institutions. According to the most recently published data, in 2011 total deposits held in these institutions by corporations, individuals, and other entities amounted to 80.9 trillion yuan ($13.3 trillion)—70 percent more than China's gross domestic product (GDP). (In the United States in 2014, M2—consisting of total demand deposits, savings deposits, and small time deposits—was 35 percent less than US GDP.)

If and when full yuan convertibility occurs, a significant share of these yuan balances (perhaps 10 percent or more) will diversify into other foreign assets, especially dollar assets. Buying up foreign assets on a major scale means flooding the market with yuan, putting downward pressure on its value.

And as long as China maintains an annual current account surplus—currently about $190 billion—some of it will further boost demand for foreign assets, thereby further weakening the yuan's exchange rate.

These three factors mean that the yuan's value is likely to stabilize toward the lower end of the sixteen to twenty cents range. That said, so long as China's unusually high savings rate persists—about 40 percent of GDP compared with less than 10 percent in the United States—so too will large surpluses recur in its current account.

The relationship between savings and the current account balance follows because of how the components of each are defined: the excess of domestic savings above domestic investment equals the excess of current earnings from abroad above payments to foreign recipients. But this accounting relationship doesn't say what's causing what. The yuan's equilibrium value will reflect the relationship; it doesn't cause it.

China's current account surpluses will shrink if and as domestic consumption rises and saving falls relative to domestic investment. How this change affects China's economic growth will depend as much on how efficiently investment is allocated as on the increase in consumption. The yuan's exchange rate will accompany and adjust to these changes, rather than drive them, and the accusations of currency manipulation will fall by the wayside.

POSTAUDIT

Written early in 2014, this essay summarizes the argument made in Chapter 7: a market-based exchange rate for China's yuan is likely to depreciate, toward the lower end of a range between sixteen and twenty US cents per yuan or slightly below it. *Score: Good*

11 Developmental Corruption in China

Charles Wolf Jr. on Double Paradox:
Rapid Growth and Rising Corruption
in China *by Andrew Wedeman*

Economists occasionally feel called on to correct, or at least modify, conclusions reached by political scientists, sociologists, or other members of the putatively "softer" social sciences. Examples of this hubristic role abound. For instance, the conventional wisdom among social scientists in bygone days was that "pay-as-you-go" Social Security would encourage household savings—economists correctly predicted the opposite effect. Aid to Families with Dependent Children was enacted with the conventional expectation that this entitlement would promote stability in poor families—instead, it had the opposite effect, in accord with what economic theory would predict. Also, several decades ago when the Soviet Union sought to expand its imperial reach by spreading largesse around the world, foreign policy wonks worried about the fearful consequences of this effort—economists

This article was previously published as Charles Wolf Jr., "Developmental Corruption in China," *Policy Review*, February 1, 2013, http://www.hoover.org /research/developmental-corruption-china.

provided empirical evidence that, instead, the effort was costing the Soviets more than it was worth.

Andrew Wedeman, a political scientist at the University of Nebraska, has accomplished a reversal of this pattern. His *Double Paradox* is a carefully reasoned and empirically grounded analysis of corruption in China, which runs counter to prior, frequently cited work by economists. The initial motivation, he tells us, for his long immersion in the subject of corruption sprang from economists' work in the mid-1990s that indicated that corruption exacted a measurable cost in forgone economic growth—in other words, corruption hindered growth. Instead, Wedeman's own substantial experience in China was, to the contrary, that corruption and growth thrived together: Corruption worsened as growth prospered. The economists were evidently missing something. The book's title (including its subtitle, *Rapid Growth and Rising Corruption*) reflects Wedeman's efforts to resolve this puzzle.

Wedeman defines corruption simply as "the improper use of public authority for private gain or advantage," and the book's title represents his "attempt to reconcile the double paradox of rapid growth and intensifying corruption."

To keep matters in balance, it's worth pointing out that his attempted reconciliation doesn't exactly refute the prior economic work that motivated his study. That prior work—a rigorous, cross-sectional, and time-series analysis by economist Paolo Mauro— found a statistically significant negative relationship between corruption (measured in several different ways) and aggregate investment as a fraction of gross domestic product. Measured across time and across countries, higher levels of corruption were correlated with significantly lower rates of investment. However, the direct relationship between corruption and economic growth (as distinct from the relation between corruption and investment) was, according to this prior work, not statistically significant.

While the investment rate surely affects growth (so if higher corruption lowers investment, growth might be expected to suffer as well), growth and investment are not equivalent. Indeed, later studies suggest that other things—for example, technology, innovation, entrepreneurship, and human capital (as distinct from physical investment)—are at least as important as the investment rate in affecting economic growth. If, for example, in post-Maoist, reformist China corruption actually facilitated innovation and entrepreneurship (elements of human capital that were impermissible and indeed prosecutable during Mao's Cultural Revolution of the 1960s), the expected result might well be higher growth notwithstanding a lower investment rate. Hence, Wedeman's reconciliation between corruption and growth is not fully dispositive of the prior work that motivated his own, although he assuredly registers on the other side of that divide.

The first third of *Double Paradox* deals with the generic distinction between "developmental corruption" and "degenerative corruption." Developmental corruption, according to Wedeman and exemplified by his case studies of Japan, Korea, and Taiwan, evolved as a coalition between a politically dominant entity, on the one hand (in Japan, the Liberal Democratic Party; in Korea's erstwhile days, the military; in Taiwan, the Kuomintang), and pro-growth business interests, on the other. Sustaining these coalitions in these three countries was an implicit—and sometimes explicit—understanding that the politically dominant group would implement pro-growth policies sought by business and that these emergent business interests would compensate the politicians with ample funding to support and continue their dominance of government. Development and corruption prospered together.

The result of this developmental corruption was a protracted period of both political stability and sustained economic growth in the three countries, including the lengthy tenure of the politically favored ally in each country—until recent years. The political machines in these countries became in effect development machines; hence, they were the vehicles of developmental corruption.

By way of contrast, degenerative corruption (alternatively termed predatory corruption or simply kleptocracy), extracts a toll, typically a large and increasing one, irrespective of whether the economy is growing, stagnant, or impoverished, and without regard for enacting policies to promote economic growth or to avoid policies that would hinder it. For this type of corruption, think of plunder, piracy, extortion, or Chicago gangsterism. *Double Paradox* includes vignettes of degenerative corruption exemplified by Zaire, Haiti, the Dominican Republic, Sierra Leone, the Central African Republic, and perhaps the most egregious of all, Equatorial Guinea.

The book then shifts to concentrate on corruption in China, with exhaustive details of the similarities and differences between China and the other cases covered in the previous chapters. This part of the book is an exposition, as the familiar phrase might put it, of corruption with Chinese characteristics.

China didn't have to develop a political machine to propel growth from the top down (as in Japan, Korea, and Taiwan) because it already had a formidable one in the Communist Party. In the post-Mao era, propelling growth was at the top of the party's agenda from the inception of Deng Xiaoping's reforms in the late 1970s and continuing into the present. At the start of this reformist era, corruption was only sporadic and decentralized; it was not "entrenched," according to Wedeman. Reforming the planned economy in the direction of a more market-based system provided the incentives and drivers for accelerating growth, as well as opening up abundant opportunities for new and lucrative forms of corruption.

At the core of the ensuing corruption, according to Wedeman's account, was the "dual-track price system": the transition away from prices prescribed by the planned economy and toward prices increasingly determined by competitive markets. This reformist process affected prices of commodities, investments, land, construction, and notably the prices at which government assets were sold by officialdom (including, of course, members of the Communist Party's hierarchy) to market-based buyers. These buyers included both private, commercial businesses and state-owned enterprises, which themselves experienced varying degrees of privatization through equity sales to private, nongovernment buyers.

In all of these transactions, arbitraging between the lower controlled prices and the higher market prices afforded lucrative opportunities for rent-seeking behavior by the participants. One might add that this process foreshadowed a similar one in the 1990s in Russia, when assets of the defunct Soviet Union were auctioned to preferred buyers at preferred prices, giving rise to Russia's notorious oligarchs.

In China, the ensuing corruption was contemporaneous with dramatic economic growth that, like the corruption, was also generated by reform toward a more market-based economy. Therein is the essence of Wedeman's resolution of the double paradox: the same reformist process that engendered rapid growth via the market mechanism was also the root source of rising corruption (hence, the book's subtitle). Marketized reform was the engine propelling both growth and corruption.

Wedeman's successful demonstration of the compatibility between rapid growth and rising corruption is not, however, the same as saying that the interactions between the two are equivalent in both directions. Rapid growth through transition to a more marketized economy enlarges the fare on which corruption can feed. Furthermore, even if the effect of this were to reduce the effective rate of investment (recall the prior reference to Paolo Mauro's work on corruption and investment) or to lower the productivity of investment, a relatively high rate of economic growth might persist and indeed continued to do so. Such has been China's record thus far. Whether it will endure remains to be seen.

Wedeman next focuses on the measurement of corruption and of China's anticorruption efforts. His attempts at quantifying corruption are original and informative if only partly successful. In the process he introduces such concepts as the "revealed rate of corruption" (RRC), consisting of the number and gravity of corrupt deeds that are detected and prosecuted; the "actual rate of corruption" (ARC) which, in principle, is the full extent of corruption (the iceberg of which RRC is the top); and the gap between the two, which he presumes to be dependent on "the intensity of enforcement." While the ARC and the gap between it and the RRC are unobservable, Wedeman avers that variations in them can be inferred from the time periods "when the authorities launched anti-corruption campaigns." These periods are well known because they've periodically been highly publicized. Cleverly, if not entirely convincingly, he then uses the ratio between RRC and ARC during the relatively high-intensity enforcement periods to help in estimating the "emerging rate of corruption" (ERC) and the "cumulative level of corruption" (CLC).

Most readers are as likely to be put off as to be engaged by the somewhat contrived character of these constructs. Nevertheless, the use he makes of them is of interest. Partly through their use, partly without it, Wedeman presents data from 1980 through 2008 on a range of corruption indicators including the numbers of cases of economic crimes detected and prosecuted, the levels and numbers of officials involved in corruption cases, and the financial scale of these cases. The takeaway from his analysis of these indicators is that although "the surge [in corruption] began after the advent of reform, it was not until the early 1990s that high-level corruption began to intensify."

In effect, this is the empirical validation of *Double Paradox:* according to Wedeman's time-series data, rising corruption and rapid growth moved in tandem.

Wedeman's discussion of anticorruption efforts adopts Gary Becker's rational choice model in which the prevalence of corruption depends on the difference between a perpetrator's expected value of committing a corrupt act, on one hand, and the expected value of remaining honest, on the other. In turn, the expected value of committing the corrupt act is the act's payoff, less the probability of getting caught times the severity of punishment. Thus, more rigorous enforcement that increases the probability of apprehension, or increases the severity of punishment, will reduce corruption. With respect to the latter, Wedeman concludes from what he asserts are comparable samples of criminals apprehended for corrupt acts in China and in the United States that the sentences meted out in China were "exponentially harsher than those handed down in the United States."

Despite this perhaps arguable finding, his journey through a labyrinth of Chinese data on corruption cases, criminals, and penalties over several decades leads to a balanced if inconclusive judgment that there is "little evidence that the extent of corruption has dramatically increased . . . but there is also little sign that corruption has decreased in recent years." The recent blatant evidence of egregious corruption surrounding the Bo Xilai scandals in Chongqing and elsewhere in China casts some doubt on this conclusion.

Finally, returning to what I referred to earlier as "corruption with Chinese characteristics" suggests a fundamental question: Is the relationship between the two parts—growth and corruption—symbiotic or parasitic? How this question is answered is both timely and important: timely because of the current and impending slowdown of 2 to 3 percent or more in China's growth rate; important because different answers have very different policy implications.

If the relationship is symbiotic, then growth in the past, powered by marketization, enlarged the pie on which corruption could feed, and this will continue in the future; and corruption, while facilitating growth in the past through the arbitraged movement from controlled prices to market prices, will also continue to facilitate growth in the future.

If the relationship is parasitic, then corruption extracts a toll from growth that, although not worrisome when growth was high, may become increasingly burdensome and contentious as growth declines in the future.

Mao formulated a parable to dismiss the question rather than answer it. Said he, "There is no need to squeeze all the toothpaste out of the tube [i.e., cadre corruption], you can't get it all anyway, so why bother?"

In recent conversations with friends at fairly high ranks (Levels 4 and 5 in the multitier levels of the Chinese Communist Party's aspirationally classless hierarchy), I've encountered a perspective that's quite different from Mao's dismissive one. Moreover, this current perspective adds a political dimension to the corruption-growth dichotomy, a dimension viewed by its protagonists as overriding the other two.

The tenor of this perspective can be summarized in the form of a syllogism:

- Rising and conspicuous corruption is a serious threat to the legitimacy and continuity of the Chinese Communist Party.
- As long as the state plays a major role in the economy, incentives for party members to engage in corrupt practices will be lucrative and irresistible.
- Therefore, the state should retreat and withdraw from the economy, regardless of whether withdrawal would help or hinder future growth.

The inference from this syllogism is a paradox no less striking than the two paradoxes of Wedeman's book. In effect, some staunch and aggressive Chinese Communist Party members are vigorous and articulate advocates of a more thoroughly marketized economy and a diminished and minimal economic role for the state.

To be sure, this is not the only position currently discussed among China's elite, nor is it necessarily the dominant one. Confronting a significant slowdown in China's remarkably rapid growth of the past three decades, some influential voices have recently urged an expansion of public investment and an enlarged role for the already strong state-owned enterprises, at the expense of private business. Because *Double Paradox* emphasized the boost to corruption resulting from the transition to a marketized economy and the ensuing arbitraging between controlled and market-driven prices, it is especially worthwhile to call attention to the fact that a move in the opposite direction that would enlarge the state's economic role is no less (and in some ways probably even more) prone to lead to corrupt practices.

A case in point is the so-called Chongqing model of development and the Bo Xilai scandal referred to above that followed in the wake of this megacity's model. The model consisted of a huge expansion of public investment for housing, urban infrastructure, and reforestation—all financed by municipal bonds and vigorously advocated by the city's populist mayor and former Politburo member, recently expelled from the Communist Party, Bo Xilai. Chongqing's economic growth burgeoned in the short run, accompanied by heavy tolls exacted by the mayor's family and other members of his entourage from construction contracts and by a massive accumulation of debt by the city itself.

Generalizing from this case, I'd suggest that public investment, which is ungoverned by competitive bidding, typically unmediated by market pricing, and nontransparent to outsiders, constitutes an invitation to misallocate resources and misfeasance by those overseeing the process.

If the move from a planned to a market economy in the 1980s and 1990s opened the way for a surge of corruption, an attempted reversal toward a more state-centered economy would be even more rife with corruption in the coming decade. When opportunities for corrupt practices are accessible, their curtailment depends on a rule of law that is overseen by an independent and uncorrupted judiciary. These institutions are yet to be developed in China.

POSTAUDIT

My favorable review of Wedeman's *Double Paradox* raises a few questions and criticisms along the way. Wedeman's subject is especially timely in light of the severe anticorruption drive currently being pursued by President Xi Jinping. *Score: Good*

PART II
US Economy and Other Issues

12   Where Keynes Went Wrong

*What If Government Spending
Depresses instead of Stimulates?*

It is generally recognized that the conceptual underpinnings for so-called stimulus programs lie in the theory developed by John Maynard Keynes in the 1930s. That the practical results of these programs in recent years have been negligible, if not negative, while their costs have been high may be sufficient grounds for avoiding them in the future.

But what if the theory itself is flawed? For many economists, flawed theory would be a greater concern—surely more hurtful to professional pride—than ineffectual results from programs based on a valid theory. Moreover, it would mean no amount of effort to improve the design of stimulus programs is likely to help.

Before addressing questions about the theory, let's briefly recap the costs and results of the stimulus so far.

Total stimulus costs have been high, but reckoning them accurately isn't easy. They include $787 billion in federal spending that was legislated and appropriated in 2009 with the "stimulus" label attached to it. In addition, a proper accounting of the cost

This article was previously published as Charles Wolf Jr., "Where Keynes Went Wrong: What If Government Spending Depresses instead of Stimulates?" *Weekly Standard,* November 7, 2011, http://www.weeklystandard.com/articles/where -keynes-went-wrong_604176.html.

should include several other programs and outlays that, while not carrying the "stimulus" label, were designed to boost domestic spending or preclude reductions in spending that were otherwise expected to occur. These other programs include the following: TARP (Troubled Asset Relief Program) funding to relieve the impaired asset values and weakened balance sheets of financial institutions ($700 billion), bailout funds provided to support the auto industry ($17 billion), extension of unemployment benefits to support income and spending by unemployed workers ($34 billion), and temporary subsidies for the "cash for clunkers" program ($3 billion).

These other measures should be included in a full reckoning of stimulus costs because of their shared common purpose: to boost aggregate demand or avoid its further decline as a consequence of the Great Recession.

All these outlays, amounting to more than $1.5 trillion, are properly encompassed in Keynes's central policy prescription: aggressively use public policy to stimulate "aggregate demand." Those who have criticized the government's stimulus efforts for being too small may not realize how large they have actually been.

What about the results of the stimulus package? Between the end of the second quarter of 2009 (when, incidentally, the Great Recession's two-year negative gross domestic product [GDP] trend ended) and the end of the second quarter of 2011, nearly all the stimulus funding was disbursed. The result was that GDP increased from $12.6 trillion (in 2005 prices) to $13.3 trillion—an increase less than half the dollar-for-dollar injection of stimulus money! In the same period, gross private consumption rose by $400 billion, and gross private (nonresidential) fixed investment rose by $155 billion. In the same period, employment *decreased* by 581,000.

A simple accounting of costs and benefits—costs are high, benefits much lower—warrants skepticism about further recourse to stimulus spending. Still, it could be contended that, if the programs were better designed and better targeted in the future, results might justify the effort notwithstanding the recent record. This possibility warrants another look at the underlying Keynesian theory.

The core of the theory is "aggregate demand" defined in terms of two components: consumption demand and investment demand. In defining and measuring these components, Keynes acknowledged, with unusual and becoming modesty, his debt to a contemporary, the Russian-American academic Simon Kuznets, who pioneered the development of a national accounting framework, which Keynes used in formulating his general theory. (Kuznets received the Nobel Prize in Economics in 1971; Keynes died before the prize, which is not awarded posthumously, was initiated.)

Insufficient aggregate demand was Keynes's diagnosis of the Depression-era conditions of continued unemployment and stagnant economic growth. Consumption demand had sharply contracted owing to the Great Depression's effect on employment and income, and investment demand was depressed because profitable investment opportunities depended heavily on consumption, which had been decimated by the Depression.

Keynes's prescription for escaping this vicious circle was to stimulate aggregate demand by aggressively increasing government spending, lowering taxes, or doing both. Unlike many of his current disciples, Keynes acknowledged the potential of lower taxes to stimulate demand. However, the room for remedial action through tax reductions was limited in the 1930s because prevailing taxes were already low. Consequently, in Keynes's view, increased government spending was necessary to boost aggregate demand—what was referred to in that day as "pump priming" and these days as "stimulus."

Moreover, whether the stimulus was to be provided by public works ("infrastructure"), by employing workers to dig holes and then fill them, or by other means didn't matter to the theory. With ample idle resources—specifically, unemployed labor and idle plant and equipment—it was assumed that the only missing ingredient was sufficient demand to jump-start the economy. One dollar of additional government spending would wend its way through the economy as first-round recipients spent most of what they received; second-round recipients, in turn, spent most of what they received, thereby raising the income and ensuing spending of the next recipients; and so on. The total effect would thus be a multiple of the initial increase in spending. If, for example, the proportion of government's increased spending that was spent by recipients was, say, 50 percent, the multiplier effect through the full economic circuit would be $2 for each dollar of increased spending; if the proportion were 60 percent, the multiplier would be 2.5.

The similarities between the Depression era and the current circumstances of our post–Great Recession are obvious. So where's the flaw?

All economic theories involve assumptions. The critical question is whether the assumptions are realistic. If there is uncertainty about the answer, the follow-on question is, How much will it matter if the assumptions are wrong?

Keynes assumed that the initial deficient level of aggregate demand would remain unchanged until the stimulative ("pump priming") effect of additional government spending kicked in. In other words, increased government spending, or its anticipation, would not further diminish preexisting levels of consumer demand and investment demand. However, Keynes's failure to consider the possibility of an adverse effect from government spending—that it might lead to still further decay in the prior levels of consumption and investment—was a fundamental flaw in the theory.

So how might government spending actually undermine its explicit purpose of boosting aggregate demand?

It is quite plausible that the behavior of consumers and investors might change as an unintended consequence of the increased government spending and might do so in ways that would partly, fully, or even more than fully offset the attempted effort to raise aggregate demand.

Consider "Ricardian equivalence"—a conjecture advanced by David Ricardo a century before Keynes's general theory and thus something Keynes was aware of or should have been aware of. Ricardian equivalence suggests that consumers might reduce their spending to prepare for the tax increases they'd face in the future to pay for government spending financed by borrowing in the present. In recent years, Ricardo's conjecture has been applied and tested in a formal model developed by Robert Barro.

That prior consumption demand might actually have been reduced as a result of recent government stimulus spending is suggested by two indicators: since mid-2009, household savings *increased* by 2–3 percent of GDP, and household debt *decreased* by 8.6 percent ($1.1 trillion).

It is also plausible that investment demand might shrink as a result of increased government spending or its anticipation. This diminution might occur if investors have recourse to other investment opportunities that seem more profitable or less risky than those that would accompany or follow the attempted government stimulus. For example, such opportunities might lie in investing abroad where tax liabilities are less onerous rather than investing at home, or investors might choose to invest in long-term instruments (thirty-year US government bonds) while reducing investment in fixed capital or equities. These opportunities might seem rosier because of anticipated increases in future taxes or because of increased regulatory restrictions that might (and did) accompany the increased government spending. In fact, such alternative investment opportunities are much more numerous and accessible now than in Keynes's era.

Failure to consider the potentially adverse effect of government spending on the preexisting level of aggregate demand was and remains a disabling flaw in Keynesian theory—then and now. If the theory's underlying logic is flawed, it can be expected that policies and programs based on it will fail. They have in the past. They should be avoided in the future.

POSTAUDIT

This critique of Keynesian theory seems even more convincing now in light of the slow pace of recovery from the 2008 Great Recession than when written in 2011 and more compelling than the "print-money, spend-more" arguments of such neo-Keynesian enthusiasts as Paul Krugman and Joseph Stiglitz. *Score: Good*

13   Pro-growth Austerity

Tightening the Government's Belt Doesn't
Have to Squeeze the Economy

Austerity and growth are increasingly viewed as opposites: if one is selected, the other must be sacrificed. Policies to promote growth require that austerity in government spending be forgone, while policies that impose austerity in government spending do so at the cost of growth.

The inescapability of this trade-off is a firm conviction in much of Europe's southern tier ("Club Med") and an emergent belief in the United States. Notwithstanding these constituencies, the belief is wrong. It is based on the simplistic assumption that vigorous recovery from a deep economic recession depends on boosting the amount of total spending—so-called aggregate demand—regardless of the sources and types of this aggregate (whether government or private), how they are financed (by debt or by equity, by accumulated balances or by pension funds), and the differing consequences that may thereby ensue.

If, instead, the focus shifts from aggregate demand to *disaggregating* demand into some of its components and examining the differing benefits and costs that are associated with these

This chapter was previously published as Charles Wolf Jr., "Pro-growth Austerity: Tightening the Government's Belt Doesn't Have to Squeeze the Economy," *Weekly Standard*, July 2, 2012, http://www.weeklystandard.com/articles/pro -growth-austerity_647784.html.

components, it is evident that there are many fruitful ways of galvanizing growth while austerely confining government spending. Austerity and growth can in fact complement one another.

Take, for example, the widespread, bipartisan agreement that the US infrastructure is badly in need of upgrading and maintenance. Our roads, highways, bridges, ports, and airports are embarrassingly shoddy compared with what we experience in traveling abroad (including in many lower-income countries). At the same time as there is a dearth of infrastructure upgrades, the balance sheets of corporate America are leavened by more than $2 trillion of cash balances, and the nation's banks hold $1.5 trillion excess reserves, about five times their holdings prior to the recession in 2008. So abundant liquidity and investable capital are available in US financial and nonfinancial institutions to finance promising, profitable ventures.

If we were to allow for, encourage, and assure the use of tolls and fees to repay investors, the large pool of available liquidity could provide ample commercial funding of infrastructure improvements, without debt-financed government spending. The process could be given a further lift by using a portion of existing highway-tax revenues along with prospective tolls as components of new derivative financial instruments to hedge investors' risks.

Next, consider education. Annual US spending for K–12 schooling is more than $600 billion—mainly consisting of spending by states and districts, supplemented by $26 billion of spending by the federal government. With fifty-three million students enrolled, per capita K–12 spending is nearly $12,000 annually. Issuing vouchers to parents for, say, 10 percent less than this amount per student to be used at the parents' choice of public, private, charter, parochial, or online schooling can plausibly—not easily but plausibly—be used to achieve both a modest increase of austerity in the public sector and a valuable stimulus to competition, innovation, and enhancement of educational quality, together producing a fillip for future economic growth.

Another example of where and how austerity and growth can be successfully combined is tax reform. It's evident that even a modest tax reform would open myriad opportunities for imposing austerity on government spending while stimulating growth. Until recently, Japan had the world's highest corporate tax rate. Now that Japan has lowered its rate, the 35 percent US rate is the highest among the world's large economies.

Grant that many and probably most American companies avoid paying this rate by retaining some of their earnings abroad or by internal transfer pricing between foreign affiliates or subsidiaries and domestic parent firms. Still, as a consequence of this avoidance strategy, US gross domestic product is lower and its growth slower than would be the case under a lower rate. Notwithstanding the slow pace of the US recovery, the United States remains the world's largest capital exporter. In 2010, US private business investment abroad was $329 billion, motivated in part by corporate tax rates that are lower abroad than at home. This outward-bound investment is equal to about 20 percent of private US domestic investment and contributes to growth elsewhere that could be happening in this country.

Think back for a moment to the bygone days of the GATT (General Agreement on Tariffs and Trade). Suppose the United States were to propose something that might be called a Most Tax-Favored Nation Treatment (MTFNT). The result of our lowering corporate tax rates to the lowest rates prevailing abroad would likely be to reduce the $329 billion outflow and to attract additional foreign capital to invest in the United States. Economic growth here would be spurred. Tax revenues might fall or rise (rates would be lower, but the amount of taxable earnings from foreign investment in the United States would rise), but no additional government spending need ensue.

Again, we would achieve austerity in debt-financed government spending, while giving an added push to economic growth: think of it as a "trade-on," rather than "trade-off."

Finally, focus again on the disaggregated components of demand rather than on the aggregate, which is the root of the mistaken view that austerity and growth are antonyms. The component parts suggest another opportunity for reinforcing the positive relation between austerity and growth.

Debt-financed government spending often has perverse effects on private consumption and private investment. Consumers may respond to additional government outlays by a precautionary rise in savings as a cushion for anticipated higher taxes required to service the added debt in the future. Investors may also worry lest the increase in government spending adversely affect their business planning (for example, the added government spending might help competing producers, or subsidize competing products, or be accompanied by additional regulation that would further inhibit business planning).

As a result, potential investors may respond by deferring or diminishing their otherwise intended investment. In the Keynesian vernacular, the "multiplier" may in fact turn out to be negative: the consequence of relaxing government austerity would thus be reduced economic growth.

The takeaway point from all the above is that government austerity and economic growth are not antonyms: austerity in debt-financed government spending complements economic growth rather than conflicting with it.

POSTAUDIT

The argument advanced here reinforces and expands the critique of Keynesian economics in Chapter 12 and suggests how and why austerity in government spending can promote rather than inhibit economic growth. *Score: Good*

14 Explaining the Recovery's Puzzles

Recent reports of the US economy's recovery pose a couple of puzzles that are likely to recur in the coming months.

The first puzzle juxtaposes two seemingly contradictory statistics: the first, an encouragingly large reduction in the rate of unemployment (from 9.8 percent to 9.4 percent) in January 2011; the second, a discouragingly small increase in new jobs created (about thirty-five thousand) in the same period. The seeming contradiction is that the percentage decline (0.4 percentage point) in unemployment corresponds to about six hundred thousand jobs—seventeen times larger than the actual number of new jobs created. The contradiction is explained by the fact that a decline in recorded unemployment may occur not only because of new jobs created and filled but also for other reasons: for example, withdrawals from the labor market after protracted and unsuccessful job search, inclement weather that inhibits job search, return to school after temporary employment, or withdrawals by immigrant workers from unemployment records.

The second puzzle is that the high rate of US unemployment has been accompanied by a rate of annualized gross domestic product (GDP) growth currently exceeding 3 percent—about twice that of other developed economies in the European Union and Japan, although still modest compared to growth in China and India.

The puzzle presented by relatively high economic growth occurring while high unemployment persists is explained by a striking rise in labor productivity.

Between the beginning of the recession in 2008 and the present, nonfarm business productivity increased at an annual rate of more than 4.3 percent. Real GDP, which had fallen by 6 percent in the recession, has now reached a level slightly above its prerecession peak. During this period, recorded unemployment rose by about 5 percent. If further allowance is made for furloughed, part-time, and temporary labor, as well as workers who withdrew from the labor force, actual unemployment (as distinct from recorded unemployment) has risen by at least 10 percent.

In effect, aggregate output in the US economy is now above its prerecession peak, with 10 percent less labor employed in producing it!

Although it's not unusual for productivity to rise during and following recessions, productivity increases in prior recoveries have been much less than the recent experience. The surprising scale of recent productivity increases is due to a combination of vigorous cost cutting, more efficient management, lower costs of borrowing, improved technology, and a spate of mergers, acquisitions, and sell-offs that streamline overhead, production, and distribution.

These productivity-enhancing measures have been propelled by vigorous supply-side competition—from both domestic and foreign sources—and by demand-side pressure from consumers who have become more cost conscious, more selective in their purchases, and more inclined to save as a consequence of the recession's duration and duress.

In turn, the productivity boom translates into rising corporate earnings, stronger US competitiveness, rising exports, and an improving if volatile S&P 500.

While employment will increase as a consequence of this good news, the bad news is that increases in employment may well be limited and selective. Employers will impose a productivity threshold on new hires sufficient to sustain the rising trends of profits and competitiveness. Hence, unemployment is likely to remain higher than that experienced in prior recoveries. Near-term, recorded unemployment between 8 and 9 percent is likely to persist.

Options for mitigating this bad news are numerous, as well as uncertain in their costs and consequences. The options include further "stimulus" programs now rendered most unlikely because of their previous ineffectiveness and overriding pressures to cut government budgets and reverse huge and still-growing federal deficits.

Another option is formal education and training designed to enhance skills and work habits, thereby enabling recipients to meet the higher bar of enhanced productivity standards. A promising but often neglected type of training can be provided on the job by many companies and businesses with effects on productivity that may exceed as well as complement those provided by formal educational institutions. On-the-job-derived skills can provide a significant portion of what is required for current and later success. Incentives for the private sector to undertake and enhance such programs tailored for new hires might be provided through tax credits that would lower their costs.

Still another venue for productive employment resides in community-building activities, whether faith based, school based, museum based, art based, or recreation based. The need for expanding such activities is obvious, given that the workload of volunteers who currently perform the bulk of these activities is typically hugely overburdened.

Funding for these options is admittedly problematic. Government funding is unlikely because of already soaring public deficits and accumulated debt. But a system of calibrated tax credits might provide incentives for companies to expand on-the-job training for new hires to enable them to reach the higher productivity bar. Finally, philanthropy may be a source of additional funding for community-building jobs if emerging tax reforms continue to encourage charitable giving. Philanthropic funding can be designed to encourage such jobs without adversely affecting similar ongoing services that are now mostly provided by uncompensated volunteers.

Absent ingenuity and progress along these lines, what impends is not a "jobless" recovery—which implies zero job increases—but a distinctly "less-jobs" recovery.

POSTAUDIT

Part of the prognosis from this March 2011 essay has been validated (fewer jobs were generated during the recovery than in prior recoveries), and part has not been (productivity increased less in 2012–2014 than in 2009–2011). And the so-called polarization of employment that has occurred—increases in higher-skilled and lower-skilled employment and shrinkage in mid-skilled employment—was not anticipated. *Score: Medium*

15 The Fed and Inequality

Zero Interest Rates Have Side Effects

Income inequality in the United States has been increasing for a generation. The share of pretax income received by the top 1 percent of earners rose from 7.8 percent in 1973 to 17.4 percent in 2010. A broader and widely used measure of inequality—the Gini coefficient—indicates that inequality for the entire range of income recipients rather than only the top 1 percent has risen by 26 percent since the early 1970s.

A caveat: These indicators, and most other indicators of inequality—and virtually all public commentary about it—relate to income before taxes. Income inequality after taxes is substantially diminished because of the offsetting effects of taxation. Specifically, the top 1 percent of income recipients pay 37 percent of total tax revenues, and the top 5 percent and 20 percent pay 59 percent and 70 percent, respectively. The bottom 50 percent pay little or no income taxes.

Pretax income inequality has been driven by long-term societal trends that are numerous, complex, and hard to change. Although the drivers are well known, their relative strength is not.

This article was previously published as Charles Wolf Jr., "The Fed and Inequality: Zero Interest Rates Have Side Effects," *Weekly Standard*, February 17, 2014, http://www.weeklystandard.com/articles/fed-and-inequality_778822.html.

They include education, parenting and family structure, neighborhood, immigration, globalization, and information technology, which often substitutes fewer high-skilled and higher-salaried workers who are fewer in number in place of more numerous and lower-paid labor. Another of the long-term trends is the inertial effect of poverty itself—poverty typically and strongly impedes emergence from it. These drivers continue to affect income inequality in the United States, as well as in many other countries.

Adding to the long-term drivers and providing a neglected and unexpected but significant boost to rising inequality in recent years has been the Federal Reserve's pursuit of sharply eased monetary policy. Conceived as a necessary means to stimulate the economy and accelerate the slow pace of recovery from the Great Recession, eased monetary policy (or quantitative easing) injected as much as $4 trillion into the monetary base by Federal Reserve purchases of mortgage-backed securities to lower long-term interest rates while maintaining near-zero short-term rates through control of the Federal Funds rate. The result has been an increase in income inequality in recent years as an unintended side effect of monetary easing, apart from and additional to the long-term trends mentioned earlier. That's because this monetary policy has induced rapid growth of profits while wages stagnated, hence an increased share of profits and a reduced share of wages in gross national income.

The process has been accompanied by a surge of equity markets to record highs (up 30 percent in 2013); burgeoning initial public offerings; heightened activities of hedge funds, private equity funds, and venture capital financing; and a generalized boom in the financial services industry. Managers of these financial endeavors are uniquely equipped to nimbly deploy the low interest rates in ways that boost the profitability of their activities. As a result, the financial sector's annual profits increased by $200 billion between prerecession 2007 and 2013. The financial sector's profits rose from 18 percent of total corporate profits preceding the recession in 2007 to 23 percent in 2013.

Increased financial sector profits mainly accrue to upper-income recipients, who are relatively few in number, while the decreased share of wages affects the relatively larger number of workers—thus providing a strong fillip to inequality. Since the Great Recession, the share of wages in national income has decreased rapidly—from 65 percent in 2008 to 61 percent in 2013—while the corresponding share of profits has risen from 11 percent in 2008 to 15 percent in 2013. Although small in percentage terms, the shift is quantitatively large. It represents $600 billion less for the wages and salaries of the relatively numerous middle- and lower-income recipients and correspondingly more for the much less numerous profit recipients, who mainly were already higher earners. Although inequality has also increased among recipients of wages, the far smaller number of profit recipients has had a dominant effect on income inequality in recent years.

Increased inequality is not simply an unintended consequence of eased monetary policy; it is also quite remote from the prescribed mandates of the Federal Reserve: principally, market stability and, as a secondary goal policy, full employment. Those who advocate both monetary easing and reduced income inequality should be aware of the tension between them. The more one is concerned with slowing, let alone reversing, the rising pace of inequality, the sooner one should favor tapering quantitative easing. Conversely, the more one is concerned with stimulating growth, the more one should favor continued easing. The Fed's recent announcement of two successive monthly reductions in the quantity of easing is an evident move favoring reduced inequality.

Accurate measurement of inequality is itself problematic. Probably the most widely used indicator is the Gini coefficient, which measures the gap between each percentage of the population and the corresponding percentage of income (or wealth) received by that percentage. If 5 percent of the population receives 5 percent of income and all other population percentages receive the corresponding income percentages, then the Gini coefficient is 0, indicating maximum equality of income distribution and no gap between population percentages and income percentages. At the other extreme, if a single recipient were to receive all income, the Gini coefficient would be 1, representing maximum inequality.

Whether any particular level or specific change in the coefficient—either closer to or farther from equality—is "good" or "bad" cannot be inferred from the Gini number alone. This crucial inference depends on what accounts for the underlying change in the inequality number. Is the change caused by positive effects of greater work effort, higher labor productivity, innovation, entrepreneurship, improved technology, or more efficient management, or is it instead caused by the negative effects of favoritism, nepotism, collusion, bribery, fraud, insider trading, special privilege, or other forms of maleficent behavior?

For example, is increased income inequality attributable more to such positive effects as those resulting from Steve Jobs and Apple, Bill Gates and Microsoft, and Larry Page and Sergey Brin and Google or instead to negative effects such as those emanating from the likes of Ken Lay and Jeff Skilling and Enron, Dennis Kozlowski and Tyco, and Bernie Madoff and his Ponzi schemes? Quite different policy implications follow from the answer. And if the answer is neither all one nor all the other, how can the positive elements be sustained and the negative behaviors reversed? The answer to this question lies more in the realm of improving corporate governance than in changing public policy.

According to recent US census data, the Gini coefficient for the United States lies midway between .45 and .49, having risen from a low of .39 in 1968 to a high of .48 in 2011. European countries show less inequality than the United States, as do Japan, South

Korea, and Israel. The Gini coefficient estimate for China is higher than that of the United States, as is the estimate for Brazil.

These estimates are, of course, based on income before taxes. As noted earlier, after-tax income inequality is substantially less: the Gini coefficient for after-tax income in the United States is perhaps as much as 10 percentage points lower than the before-tax estimate.

It is doubtful that this large a change in the Gini indicator would be found in the after-tax estimates for most other countries. It is also doubtful that quantitative easing has had as large an effect on income inequality in other countries as it has in the United States.

POSTAUDIT

The interval between early 2014, when this article was written, and now is too short to claim much prescience. Still, the nexus between eased monetary policy and economic inequality is both more important than is usually acknowledged and largely neglected in discussions of each. *Score: Good*

16   Income Inequality

Farsighted Leadership in a Shortsighted World

CHARLES WOLF JR. AND JOHN GODGES

Income inequality, which became the principal concern of the Occupy Wall Street movement of late 2011 and much of 2012, has remained a prominent issue throughout a presidential campaign season focused on jobs, the economy, and taxes. Unfortunately, the ongoing US debate on income inequality emphasizes the magnitude of inequality and the changes in it. The debate neglects why inequality occurs, which reasons are good and which are not, and what, if anything, to do about it.

President Barack Obama argues that the US tax code has benefited the wealthy and well connected at the expense of the vast majority of Americans. His campaign asserts that a third of the four hundred highest-income taxpayers paid an average rate of just 15 percent or less in 2008. That is why he has proposed the Buffett Rule, asking millionaires and billionaires to pay their "fair share." Obama has also asked Congress to reform the tax code and to close tax loopholes for millionaires and billionaires, as well as hedge fund managers, private jet owners, and oil companies.

This chapter was previously published as Charles Wolf Jr. and John Godges, "Income Inequality: Charles Wolf, Jr., and John Godges on Isolating Its Sources," *RAND Review*, Fall 2012, http://www.rand.org/pubs/periodicals/rand-review /issues/2012/fall/leadership/income-inequality.html.

Meanwhile, he has cut taxes for middle-class families and small businesses.

The crucial question is *what accounts for* the inequality?

Governor Mitt Romney, in contrast, argues that America's individual tax code applies relatively high marginal tax rates on a narrow tax base, discouraging work and entrepreneurship, and that the country's 35 percent corporate tax rate is among the highest in the industrial world, reducing the ability of the nation's businesses to compete in the global economy. Romney promises to make a permanent, across-the-board, 20 percent cut in individual marginal tax rates; to eliminate taxes on interest, dividends, and capital gains for those with adjusted gross incomes below $200,000; to cut the corporate tax rate to 25 percent; and to repeal other taxes.

In the charged environment of the US presidential election campaign, this debate is sometimes referred to as "class warfare." The heated debate includes allusions to the role of inequality as a contributing cause of America's recession, the increased inequality that has resulted from the recession, and the extent to which increased inequality has adversely affected the pace and vigor of recovery from this recession compared with prior ones.

It is useful to consider the best single indicator of inequality: the Gini coefficient, named for the twentieth-century Italian statistician Corrado Gini. The Gini coefficient represents the gap between a percentage of the population and its corresponding percentage of income received.

If 1 percent of the population receives 1 percent of total income, and 5 percent of the population receives 5 percent of total income, and all other population percentages receive their corresponding percentages of total income—that is, if there is no gap between the population and income percentages—then the Gini coefficient is 0, representing perfect equality of incomes. If, at the other extreme, a single recipient receives all income, then the Gini coefficient hits its peak of 1, representing maximum inequality. In the real world, the country with the greatest income inequality is Namibia, where the bottom 70 percent of the population earns only 7 percent of the income and the top 30 percent earns 93 percent of the income, resulting in a Gini coefficient of .71. Sweden has one of the lowest Gini coefficients, at .23.

According to the best US government data estimating Gini coefficients around the world, the Unites States falls in the middle of the range (between .45 and .49). European countries show less inequality than the United States, as do Japan, South Korea, India, Turkey, and Israel. Several rapidly growing developing economies, including Brazil, show greater inequality.

But whether any level or change in the Gini coefficient is "good" or "bad" cannot be inferred from the coefficient alone. The crucial question is *what accounts for* the inequality? For those with more income, is it because of greater work effort, higher labor productivity, innovation, entrepreneurship, better technology, or more efficient management or, instead, to favoritism, nepotism, collusion, bribery, fraud, insider trading, special privilege, other forms of corruption, or unequal opportunity? If the explanation lies in higher productivity and better management, then the income inequality warrants encouragement. If, instead, the inequality is a result of nepotism and corruption, it should be combated and reversed. If the answer is a combination, which explanation predominates? And how can the positive factors be encouraged while the latter are reduced?

The mixed picture of income inequality around the world reinforces the basic takeaway point: it is more important to know the underlying explanations for inequality across countries and within them than the amount of inequality or changes in it. The inequality debate should focus more on the sources of and reasons for inequality and less on how much inequality there is or how much it has changed, more on explaining inequality and less on deploring or defending it.

POSTAUDIT

Pretax income inequality in the United States is moderately greater than in most European Union countries and Japan; post-tax inequality is less. Before considering whether and how to reduce inequality, we need to understand inequality's sources. More specifically, we need to understand which sources relate to productivity and which do not and focus on reducing the latter. *Score: Good*

17 One Policy Change, Please

TIE asked this question: What if you became president of the United States in January 2013 and could accomplish only one realistic policy change to restore economic growth and employment to historic trend levels? What would that policy change be?

A simpler and flatter tax system. Policy changes that will restore growth and employment and have at the same time realistic possibilities of enactment are indeed few and far between. My favorite candidate is a decisive move toward a simpler and flatter tax system.

The essential components of this change have been outlined by economists on both sides of the political spectrum. They consist of the following:

- A revenue-neutral structure would be targeted on a federal revenue level approximating 20 percent of gross domestic product.
- A rate structure would have a top bracket of 28 percent of all income sources, including salaries, bonuses, capital gains, dividends, interest, and carried interest.

This excerpt was previously published in "One Policy Change, Please," *International Economy*, Fall 2012, 31–32.

- The top tax rate would apply to corporate as well as personal income.
- No more than two lower marginal rates would apply to income below the threshold level at which the 28 percent rate kicks in (for example, the threshold could be specified as $500,000).
- A cap on allowable deductions would be set between $17,000 and $25,000 but at a sufficiently low level to assure compliance with the revenue-neutrality criterion mentioned above.

The president should accompany the legislation that establishes this simpler and flatter tax policy with a resounding affirmation of its overriding purpose. That purpose is to encourage and energize the private business sector to deploy the enormous resources it possesses to enhance growth and employment—resources that include both human talent and the ample financial liquidity presently in corporate balance sheets and the large excess reserves of the banking system. The president's pronouncement would emphasize that the government's task is to guide and constructively regulate the business environment in directions that encourage private enterprise while relying on a vigorous entrepreneurial business sector to generate growth and employment.

POSTAUDIT

This response to a symposium question—tax reform as key to boosting growth and employment in the US economy—remains important and necessary, despite being unrealistic. If Republicans gain control of the Senate in the midterm elections of 2014, prospects for tax reform are likely to brighten. *Score: Good*

18   Tax the Nonprofits

A Modest Proposal

Nonprofit organizations (NPOs), often referred to as the "independent sector," are an essential part of America's vibrant, pluralistic civil society. Their activities span a wide range of public and private purposes—philanthropic, cultural, religious, professional, educational, and scientific. The public and the private interests that NPOs represent add vitality and fractiousness to American society.

A common feature nurtured by NPOs' expansive diversity is their "enormous and incessant growth," to quote a leading authority, Bruce Hopkins.[1] Although their exact number isn't known, the best current estimate is about 2 million, consisting of 1.4 million in the annual IRS registry, an additional number of religious organizations (approximately 350,000), and a further increment of smaller NPOs. Neither religious organizations nor the smaller NPOs are required to file annual returns with the IRS—hence the uncertainty about a precise number.

This article was previously published as Charles Wolf Jr., "Tax the Nonprofits: A Modest Proposal," *Weekly Standard,* March 11, 2013, http://www.weeklystandard .com/articles/tax-nonprofits_704966.html.

Can the NPO sector contribute to easing the US fiscal imbalance while helping rather than hindering the dynamic free enterprise system and retaining societal benefits provided by nonprofits?

Annual NPO income is about $1.6 trillion—a revenue stream equal to 9 percent of US gross domestic product (GDP). This income includes donations and membership fees deductible from contributors' taxable income and earnings realized by some NPOs from services they provide to government and to the business sector. NPOs are allowed to earn income consistent with their nonprofit status but are restricted in realizing profits from such earnings and in the uses for net earnings.

Employment in the independent sector is 8–9 percent of total nonfarm civilian employment, and total assets held by NPOs are estimated at $2 trillion, about twice the amount held a decade ago.

The United States continues a slow and unprecedentedly weak recovery from the Great Recession of 2008–2009—depressingly reminiscent of Japan's protracted stagnation since 1990. Annual US GDP growth is less than 2 percent, while unemployment hovers between 7 and 8 percent. If involuntary underemployment and temporary employment are included, total unemployment is 14–15 percent of the labor force. The accompanying fiscal predicament consists of a federal budget deficit of more than $1.2 trillion in each of the past three fiscal years and an accumulated gross public debt approaching $17 trillion, which now exceeds GDP. Slightly over 70 percent of the gross debt is publicly held, and more than one-third of the publicly held debt is owed to other countries (mainly China and Japan); the government debt that's not publicly held resides mainly in the balance sheets of the Federal Reserve.

Resolving our budget problems is difficult and urgent—the difficulty is compounded by the intense wrangling that pervades the political system. While the two political parties profess agreement on the need to reduce both the annual deficit and the accumulated gross debt, the parties disagree over how large the reductions should be; whether they should be accomplished by cutting spending, by raising revenues, or by both measures; and how much of the reductions should be made now versus in the future. Invoking the future reminds us that actions taken now do not prevent legislators and presidents from reversing them later.

Democrats urge that cuts focus mainly on defense spending, that cuts in entitlement spending should be avoided, and that any other cuts should be limited lest they set back the slow recovery. They argue that more substantial cuts should be deferred until later when (and if) more robust growth resumes. Instead of such cuts, the Democrats favor additional spending for infrastructure and education and further increases in taxation of upper-income recipients beyond those enacted a few months ago to avert the fiscal "cliff."

Republicans insist on larger spending cuts now, especially reductions in escalating entitlement costs, along with commitments for further cuts in ensuing years. Republicans oppose cutting defense spending, arguing that such costs would imperil national security. They are equally opposed to any further tax increases, arguing that these would adversely affect business investment, consumer spending, economic growth, and employment.

Despite its seeming remoteness from this familiar wrangle, the independent sector might provide a modest contribution to resolving the fiscal impasse. In the 2011 edition of his authoritative work on tax-exempt NPOs, Bruce Hopkins describes the rules for granting tax exemptions as "a hodgepodge of statutory law that has evolved over nearly 100 years."[2] Nevertheless, he identifies several "rationales" for granting tax-exempt status, one of which may be relevant and useful for easing the US fiscal predicament: the specific rationale for NPOs that relates to their ability "to lessen the burdens of government" and "serve[] as an alternative to the governmental sector as a means for addressing society's problems."[3]

I suggest we retain tax exemption for only that portion of the two million NPOs that directly "serves as an alternative to the governmental sector" and can demonstrate that existing budgets of specific government agencies and programs will be reduced as a consequence of the NPOs' activities. For all the remaining NPOs, a modest excise tax (for example, 10 percent) would be levied on their income.

The fraction of NPOs that would remain tax exempt is probably small. I conjecture that perhaps 15 percent might qualify while the remainder would not—the qualifiers being only those NPOs that compete with and can substitute for government provision of services (for example, preschool and K–12 education or R&D services). The revenue enhancement that might be expected from the levy on the no-longer-tax-exempt NPOs would be about $140 billion annually—a modest but significant reduction in the overall fiscal imbalance.

In this scenario, donors' contributions to charitable organizations would remain tax-exempt for donors, although as income to the recipient NPOs, the contributions would be subject to the excise tax.

The multifaceted activities of the NPOs subject to the excise tax would obviously be scaled back, although the effect would be minimal because donors would retain their deductibility. The rich diversity that NPOs contribute to America's civil society would still flourish. To the extent that a quasi-market mechanism operates in the NPO sector, we can expect (or at least hope) that any reductions in donations and after-tax income would mainly affect the less effective NPOs. Moreover, the tax differentiation that retains an exemption for those NPOs specifically providing services that substitute for government outlays would have several worthwhile consequences: streamlining government, incentivizing NPOs to provide services that reduce government spending, and helping ease the acute US fiscal imbalance.

The short-term effects of taxing some NPOs would make a modest contribution to reducing this imbalance. Business taxes and personal income taxes would be unaffected. In the medium to longer term, the effects of differentiated taxation of NPOs would increase the scale and activity of those that compete with government and hence would tend to curtail its expansion. Although donations to the large majority of taxed NPOs would remain deductible from the donors' taxable income, the lower after-tax income of the NPOs would tend to reduce only slightly their numbers and scale.

It is also possible that the modest NPO contribution to reducing the overall fiscal imbalance could catalyze similarly modest contributions by reduced spending on entitlements and on defense. For example, Medicare spending might be modestly reduced by the introduction of scaled copayments for all nonemergency care and by nationwide, cross-state competition among insurers. Modest reductions in Social Security outlays might be accomplished by adopting an inflation index for cost-of-living allowances that takes account of quality improvements and by prudently linking outpayments from the Social Security system to inpayments made to it. And reductions in defense spending might be realized by lowering some outlays for personnel and for O&M (organization and management) rather than outlays for procurement and for RDT&E (research, development, test, and evaluation). These several sources of lower spending—each modest in size—plus the tax revenues from NPOs can sufficiently reduce the overall fiscal imbalance so that a resumption of normal GDP growth rates would entirely eliminate the imbalance!

Notwithstanding these changes, America's civil society would remain far and away the world's most diverse, vigorous, and influential.

Notes

1. Bruce R. Hopkins, *Law of Tax-Exempt Organizations,* 10th ed. (Hoboken, NJ: Wiley, 2011), 23.
2. Ibid., 9.
3. Ibid., 207, 11.

POSTAUDIT

Taxing the income of NPOs (501(c)(3), (4), and (5) organizations)—except those that demonstrate that their activities do or will commensurately reduce government spending—seems to me as meritorious (as well as unrealistic) now as it was when written two years ago. Perhaps it might be more realistic if a distinction were made between 501(c)(3) NPOs (educational and charitable organizations), which would remain tax exempt, and other NPOs (501(c)(4) and (5)), whose income would be taxed. The article neglects to make this distinction. *Score: Medium*

19 The Facts about American "Decline"

It's fashionable among academics and pundits to proclaim that the United States is in decline and no longer number one in the world. The declinists say they are realists. In fact, their alarm is unrealistic.

Early declinists like Yale historian Paul Kennedy focused in the 1980s on the allegedly debilitating effects of America's "imperial overstretch." More recently, historians Niall Ferguson and Martin Jacques focus on the weakening of the economy. Among pundits, Paul Krugman and Michael Kinsley on the left and Mark Helprin on the right sound the alarm.

The debate involves issues of absolute versus relative decline and concepts like "resilience" and "passivity." Some issues are measurable, like gross domestic product (GDP), military power, and demographics. Others are not measurable or are less measurable.

In absolute terms, the United States enjoyed an incline this past decade. Between 2000 and 2010, US GDP increased 21 percent in constant dollars, despite the shattering setbacks of the Great Recession in 2008–2009 and the bursting of the dot-com bubble

This article was previously published as Charles Wolf Jr., "The Facts about American 'Decline,'" *Wall Street Journal*, April 13, 2011, http://online.wsj.com /news/articles/SB10001424052748704415104576251292725228886.

in 2001. In 2010, US military spending ($697 billion) was 55 percent higher than in 2000. And in 2010, the US population was 310 million, an increase of 10 percent since 2000.

The notion that demography is destiny may be a stretch, but demographics are important when, as in the United States, population increase—due to higher birth and immigration rates than in other developed countries—cushions the impact of an aging population.

But there were also some important declines relative to the rest of the world. In 2000, US GDP was 61 percent of the combined GDPs of the other G20 countries. By 2010, that number dropped to 42 percent. In 2000, US GDP was slightly more than 8 times that of China, but it fell to slightly less than 3 times in 2010. Japan is a contrasting case: US GDP was 2 times as large as Japan's in 2000 but 2.6 times as large in 2010, before the tsunami and nuclear disasters of 2011.

Between the inclines and declines are other data to be considered.

In absolute terms, the United States increased its GDP, population, and military spending from 2000 to 2010. In relative terms, the story is not always as good, especially in GDP.

US military spending inclined substantially to more than 2 times that spent by all non-US NATO members in 2010 from 1.7 times in 2000; to 17 times Russian spending in 2010 from 6 times in 2000; and to 9 times Chinese spending in 2010 from 7 times in 2000.

Demographically, the US population in 2000 (282 million) was 4.6 percent of the global population; by 2010, the US population (310 million) had risen to 4.9 percent of the global figure. The US population was 59 percent as large as that of the fifteen-member European Union in 2000; that figure increased to 78 percent by 2010 (counting only 2000's fifteen members) and to 62 percent if we count the twelve new EU members added between 2004 and 2007.

The US population grew to 10 percent more than that of Japan's and 13 percent more than that of Russia's between 2000 and 2010. Relative to the huge populations of China and India (1.3 billion and 1.2 billion, respectively), the US population during the past decade increased slightly (0.16 percent) compared to China and decreased by a similar margin compared to India.

What matters more than absolute numbers is the population's composition of prime working-age people versus dependents. Compared to most developed economies and China, the US demographic composition is relatively favorable.

So what do all these numbers tell us about decline or incline?

Despite the Great Recession, the three crude indicators—GDP, military spending, and population growth—show that the US inclined in absolute terms.

But in relative terms, the picture is more complicated. Although US GDP grew substantially in real terms during the decade, relative to the G20 countries as a group US GDP declined by 19 percent. Relative to China, the US decline was even larger.

As noted, military spending by the United States increased across the board relative to NATO's, China's, and Russia's. Whether this suggests the United States is allocating too much or other countries too little is not evident from numbers alone. And numbers also don't indicate whether high military outlays have a positive or negative effect on economic growth.

As for demography, there was a small US increase relative to global population, a moderate increase relative to the European Union, large increases relative to Japan and Russia, and slight and opposite changes relative to China and India.

And there you have it: some numbers show inclines, some show declines, and some numbers are mixed. What the numbers omit is as significant as what they convey. Omissions include the societal and systemic factors that stimulate or impede creativity, innovation, entrepreneurship, and new ventures.

Numbers also ignore the effects of culture, property rights, law, and political freedom in the near and long terms. Nor do the numbers foretell how China's so-called Red Capitalism will fare in long-term competition with the multihued US prototype. As for comparing and forecasting the resilience of countries and regions, the numbers ignore more than they convey.

The overall picture is far more complex than the simple one portrayed by declinists. The real world is complicated, so a portrait in one dimension distorts rather than reflects reality.

POSTAUDIT

The demographic, economic, and defense-related data for the 2001–2010 decade were more buoyant than the corresponding data since then. Relative to economic growth and military spending in other countries, the US position has declined modestly. And the deteriorated international security environment was not foreseen in the essay. *Score: Not good*

20 An *American* Lost Decade?

Is America economically headed for a 1990s-style Japanese "lost decade" of stagnant growth?

No, America is not headed for a Japanese-style lost decade, and frankly, I've never fully understood why Japan's recession lasted so long!

That said, several principal factors characterized the Japanese scenario. Monetary policy reduced short-term interest rates to zero (as the Federal Reserve has done in the United States). The huge expansion of Japan's budget deficits was an intended "stimulus" whose effects were severely blunted because it was mainly channeled through a part of the bureaucracy—namely, the Transportation Ministry—renowned for its heavy exactions of pork, corruption, and other inefficiencies. (The limited effectiveness of the US stimulus package is another worrisome similarity between the US and Japanese cases.) The Japanese macroeconomy was decisively steered by government industrial policy that, when it no longer worked, left the economy rudderless and lacking in

This excerpt was previously published in "An *American* Lost Decade?" *International Economy,* Summer 2009, 19–20.

vitality, innovation, and entrepreneurship. A set of political and societal factors, including a homogeneous, internally cohesive population and a social and economic system marked by discipline, mutual respect, and predictability, made protracted stagnation acceptable to a surprising degree. (These characteristics are quite remote from the US system and tend to make protracted stagnation less acceptable here.)

The United States won't replicate the Japanese scenarios for many reasons. The US central bank has more adroitly managed monetary policy—for example, by reducing long-term rates in addition to short rates through massive Fed buying of Treasury notes, reducing the spread between long- and short-term rates, and discounting lower-quality commercial paper to ease credit. The United States has developed innovative programs like the Term Liquidity Guarantee Program of the FDIC (Federal Deposit Insurance Corporation) designed to lower banks' borrowing costs to help thaw a frozen credit system. Multiple stimulus packages, huge fiscal deficits, and other bailout measures are collectively having some positive effect even if none has been well designed. And finally, I believe that various forces of resilience continue to be manifest in the United States to a far greater degree than in Japan: entrepreneurial zeal, openness to start-ups, ease of entry, and "animal spirits."

POSTAUDIT

That the United States will not replicate Japan's lost decade (actually two decades!) of stagnation remains a likely prognosis, although recent data perhaps make the case less compelling than when this symposium response was written. *Score: Medium*

21 What Are the Chances the United States Becomes Energy Independent?

That the US role in global energy markets will shift dramatically from being a large net energy importer to becoming a major net energy exporter is likely; that the United States will become independent of global energy markets is fanciful!

Discussion of "energy independence" is often marred by conflation of two very separate questions: whether and how much US oil and gas production will increase as a result of fracking soft shale, and whether and when the United States will become independent of global energy markets. The answer to the first question is affirmative and large; the answer to the second is never.

Note, for example, that the United States is a major global grain exporter, although grain prices in the United States are heavily influenced by prices prevailing in global grain markets. The same is true for ferrous metals and copper, aluminum, titanium, and other nonferrous metals. Where relatively homogeneous commodities are concerned—such as grain, oil, and metals—the one-price rule will prevail, along with local price differences arising mainly from variable costs of insurance, freight, and regulation.

This excerpt was previously published in "What Are the Chances the United States Becomes Energy Independent? The Views of Seventeen Noted Thinkers," *International Economy,* Fall 2013, 44–45.

The United States is a major player in these markets; it is not "independent" of them.

Trying to forecast energy prices is especially hazardous in a world whose major producers include ones located in the volatile Middle East. That said, several strong trends suggest severe downward pressure on future energy prices. Sustained and increasing supplies from fracking in the United States are only one example. Another is application of the same technology in other countries with promising shale deposits, including China, Algeria, and Argentina. Marketing efforts in these countries are already under way by several purveyors of the technology, including BP, Chevron, and perhaps others.

A third example is the increased output of energy-related supplies coming on line from China's large-scale foreign aid and investment activities in natural resource projects in Latin America, Africa, Central Asia, Southeast Asia, and other emerging-market areas.

Economists frequently talk and teach much about price elasticity of supply (and demand)—that is, how sensitive (or responsive) is supply of a product to changes in prices. Bearing in mind the numerous current and impending changes in energy supplies mentioned above, we probably should think more about the supply elasticity of prices—that is, how sensitive (responsive) are energy prices to technology-induced changes in supply.

POSTAUDIT

This 2013 assessment of the sometimes-unclear meaning and economic consequences of possible US energy independence remains valid. *Score: Good*

22 The Geopolitics of US Energy Independence

It is possible that within a decade the United States will become an energy exporter as a result of new horizontal drilling oil exploration and shale fracking techniques, as predicted by noted energy expert Phil Verleger in the lead article of the Spring 2012 issue of *TIE*.

How would or should US foreign policy change in this new era of energy independence? Would America become less concerned with providing military security in the Middle East? What would this mean for the future of US-Israeli relations? With the European countries becoming more dependent on Russia for energy supplies (at potentially far higher costs than Americans would face) and with Russia and Germany becoming closer economic partners, what are the implications for the future of NATO? On a broader note, to what extent would US energy independence bolster isolationist foreign policy tendencies already in force in the United States?

My guess is that the assumption of energy independence is as likely to be wrong as right. Setting that caveat aside but nonetheless

This excerpt was previously published in "The Geopolitics of U.S. Energy Independence: Nine Noted Observers Offer Their Views," *International Economy*, Summer 2012, 24–25.

accepting the assumption, I think its consequences would be enormous.

For commodities that are homogeneous, as is the case for oil and gas, only a single price for each (apart from cost of insurance and freight differences) must prevail in world markets. Removing the world's largest importer (the United States) from the demand side of these two global markets and adding it to the supply side (where the United States would become in effect a nonaffiliated Organization of Petroleum Exporting Countries [OPEC] partner) will dramatically affect prices in both oil and gas markets. When further allowance is made for China's large ongoing investments to expand global oil and gas supplies (especially in Africa), oil and gas prices are likely to plummet—a 50 percent decrease from current prices would not be implausible. OPEC's breakup might well ensue as a by-product.

US foreign policy and military security concerns are not thereby likely to be diminished. Such collateral events as the following would account for our continued concerns: Iran's persistent pursuit of deliverable nuclear weapons (if not yet acquired), Saudi concerns with countering this development, the heightened concerns of other Sunni elements in the Middle East, Egypt's restiveness still further aggravated by these circumstances, and Israel's concerns about what to do and how to do it in the face of these developments. In sum, I doubt that the area will be more quiescent as a result of the sharp change in relative oil and gas prices. That said, it's as plausible that US-Israeli relations will become more harmonious in these circumstances as it is that they will become less so.

Recalling my earlier reference to the prevalence in world markets of one price for homogeneous commodities, I'd opine that Europe would become less dependent on Russian energy supplies, rather than more dependent. Oil and natural gas would become buyers' markets rather than sellers' markets. European buyers will have a suppliers' queue lining up with offers!

Finally, something of a "pivot" toward Asia may still be evident in US foreign policy after a decade. Also, the United States will have ample domestic and international reasons for adopting a somewhat less conspicuous role in world affairs. Nevertheless, isolationism will become even more remote from reality a decade hence than it is now.

POSTAUDIT

This overview of the geopolitical consequences of US energy independence given in response to a symposium question is still relevant, although some particular circumstances were completely unforeseen in 2012 (e.g., Russian seizure of Crimea, civil conflict in Ukraine). *Score: Medium*

PART III

US-China Interactions

23 All Inequality Is Not Equal

ARTHUR C. BROOKS AND
CHARLES WOLF JR.

The proposition that less income inequality is better and more is worse is both politically correct and widely accepted. It is increasingly central to the political discourse in some developing nations where soaring economic growth rates have made entire populations richer—but some citizens much richer than others.

In China, for example, trade-fueled growth has more than tripled average real per capita income since 1990, accounting for over 75 percent of poverty reduction in the entire developing world. But while celebrating this extraordinary achievement, China's President Hu Jintao's address to China's Seventeenth Party Congress in October 2007—roughly comparable to the American president's State of the Union address—raised the alarm about rising gaps between rich and poor. Indeed, he accorded equal priority to reducing inequality as to high economic growth among China's main goals. As President Hu formulated China's objectives for the next decade,

> We will improve the distribution system . . . [so] . . . a proper balance will be struck between efficiency and equity in both primary distribution and redistribution, with particular emphasis on equity

This article was previously published as Arthur C. Brooks and Charles Wolf Jr.,
"All Inequality Is Not Equal," *Far Eastern Economic Review,* June 2, 2008, 23–24.

in redistribution. . . . We will increase transfer payments, intensify the regulation of income through taxation . . . and overhaul
income distribution with a view to gradually reversing the growing
income disparity.

Does China have an "inequality problem," compared with, say,
the United States? To answer this question requires a look at the
most widely accepted and generally useful quantitative measure of
income inequality, the Gini coefficient, named for its originator,
Corrado Gini, an Italian statistician in the early twentieth century.
This number ranges between 0 (signifying "perfect," or maximum, equality) and 1 (signifying maximum inequality).

The coefficient indicates the gap between two percentages:
the percentage of the population and the percentage of income
received by each percentage of the population. If, say, 1 percent
of the population receives 1 percent of total income and all subsequent percentages of the population receive the corresponding
percentages of total income, the Gini coefficient is 0—there is no
gap between the income and the population percentages. If, at
the other extreme, all of the economy's income were acquired
by a single recipient, the gap would be maximized, and the coefficient would be 1.

If the coefficient approximates 0, income received by each individual (or family or household) would be exactly the same—each
percentage of the population would receive the corresponding
percentage of income; the system's survival would be jeopardized
by an absence of pecuniary incentives for entrepreneurship, innovation, and productivity. If, on the other hand, the coefficient
approximates 1, all of the economy's income would be acquired
by a single recipient. The system's survival would depend precari-
ously on the altruism of that single recipient, with the risk of revolution if altruism is insufficient!

America's Gini coefficient climbed to .44 from .39 between 1985 and 2005, fueling the current arguments in the United States about income inequality and perhaps favoring the political fortunes of those who advocate greater redistribution of wealth. Meanwhile, China's coefficient rose to .47 from .35 in the past five years according to the Asian Development Bank. China may be on its way to making the United States look positively egalitarian.

Contrary to conventional wisdom, however, whether any specific change in the Gini coefficient closer to or farther from equality is generally "good" or "bad" cannot be judged a priori. This judgment depends on whether the strengthened incentives toward higher productivity that might be associated with a movement toward higher inequality are offset by the aggravation of social tensions that might be associated with the same movement.

In turn, such a judgment is likely to depend critically on how and why the change in inequality has occurred rather than on the magnitude of the change. For example, whether the coefficient's change is (or is perceived to be) due to favoritism, nepotism, and corruption or instead to innovation, productivity, and entrepreneurship; whether the change is viewed as earned, fair, and legitimate or instead as connived, unfair, and illegitimate.

In any event, the concern about inequality expressed by President Hu reflects the truth of an old Chinese proverb that "inequality, rather than want, is the cause of trouble." Many an oligarch has lost his head after ignoring this point. With its vast geography, enormous population, rapid growth, and an increasing impossibility of limiting access to outside information, some observers believe China may be or may become a political tinderbox.

To ameliorate class tension through income redistribution may therefore be viewed as sensible because it will enhance prospects for political survival. This view may gain credence from the fact that most recent and violent protests against China's ruling authorities have occurred in Tibet and western Xinjiang, two of China's lowest-income provinces.

However, if an income-equalizing and redistributional approach were vigorously pursued by its top policy makers, China's rapid economic growth might slacken. As Europe has long demonstrated, and as the United States may begin to experience henceforth, income equalization strategies tend to lower entrepreneurial as well as labor incentives and can easily shave nontrivial amounts off economic growth rates.

This trade-off between increased equality and economic growth is further complicated in China because it also faces a highly expensive "modernization of national defense and the armed forces." In his litany of goals, President Hu recognized this as another powerful resource claimant, ranking it only slightly lower in priority than equality and growth.

China—known to evince no less human envy than America or Europe—may well be facing a Faustian bargain between sustaining its astounding rates of economic growth and maintaining long-term political stability. Interestingly, few analysts of China's economy have predicted any slowdown in Chinese growth rates over the coming decades, because, notwithstanding the "tinderbox" allusion above, they don't consider inequality to be as much of a political danger in China as some consider it to be in the West.

Depending on the extent to which Mr. Hu's rhetoric materializes in major redistributional policies, the alarmist scenarios we commonly hear of the United States being overtaken as the world's largest economy may become increasingly unlikely if and as China's rulers seek to placate the masses who—while growing richer—are not growing rich as quickly as the favored few.

POSTAUDIT

This essay on inequality in China and in the United States remains timely and relevant in both countries; indeed its relevance has been enhanced by the (opportunistic) attention accorded to the subject of inequality by the current leadership of both countries. *Score: Good*

24 The Inequality Debate

The United States versus China

The ongoing US debate on inequality is paralleled by one in China that is less visible and less audible but no less intense. Despite their differences, the two debates share a common characteristic: what they emphasize is less important than what they neglect. They emphasize the magnitude of inequality and changes in it. They neglect why inequality occurs, which reasons are good and which are not, and what, if anything, to do about it.

In the United States, the debate unfolds during a protracted presidential election campaign. In this charged environment, the debate is sometimes referred to as "class warfare"—a term actually used by John Maynard Keynes many years ago to characterize his opposition to it. The US debate also includes allusions to the role of inequality as a contributing cause of the recession, the increased inequality that has resulted from the recession, and the extent to which increased inequality has adversely affected the pace and vigor of recovery from this recession compared with prior ones.

In China, the inequality debate has a very different cast. It is, first of all, limited by censorship and anticipation of censorship.

This article was previously published as Charles Wolf Jr., "The Inequality Debate: The United States versus China," *International Economy,* Spring 2012, http://www .international-economy.com/TIE_Sp12_Wolf.pdf.

Consequently, much of the debate is less evident in the media than on the Internet. There it has been galvanized by what the *Economist* understates as the belief of "many people that too little of the country's spectacular growth is trickling down to them."

The debate in China has been intensified by the ostensibly more redistributive and egalitarian Chongqing model of economic development advocated by the recently dismissed Chongqing party chief Bo Xilai versus the soi-disant growth-at-any-price Guangdong model.

Another distinctive aspect of China's inequality debate is largely confined to the country's top leadership, quite apart from the Internet. This aspect consists of two additional factors: an impending reduction of 2–3 percent in China's remarkable 9–10 percent annual growth rate during the past three decades and the ongoing transition from China's ten-year leadership of Hu Jintao to the designated new leader, Xi Jinping, and his soon-to-be-named associates on the Politburo Standing Committee.

The new leadership confronts the risk that increased social unrest might result from the occurrence of rising and conspicuous inequality throughout the economy at the same time as China encounters slower economic growth. This risk is magnified by substantial inequality between China's high-income and high-growth eastern provinces and its poorer and slower-growing central and western provinces. Adding fuel to these embers is the non-Han ethnicity of some of the "less-equal" parts of the populace that inhabits some of the poorer provinces, notably in Tibet and Xinjiang.

Underlying the differing debates in the United States and China is a presumption that inequality can be reliably measured and that measurement enables useful comparisons of inequality within and between countries and across different time periods.

Measurement involves serious data problems in both the United States and China: for example, whether pretax or post-tax income is the proper metric for assessing inequality, whether the preferred metric should be confined to money income or instead should also include in-kind income, and whether nontaxed benefits (such as employer-provided health insurance) should be included as well.

Measurement problems also include a serious question of which among several candidate indicators is best for measuring inequality.

Data problems aside, the best single indicator of inequality is the Gini coefficient, named for a twentieth-century Italian statistician, Corrado Gini. While the Gini coefficient is not immune from technical criticism—it is not an elixir emanating from a magical vessel—it is the most comprehensive and familiar inequality indicator. It is the inequality indicator that is most widely used by governments and academics, including those in China, the United States, and most other countries.

The Gini coefficient shows the gap between the percentage of the population and the corresponding percentage of income (or wealth or education or any other aspect of well-being that may be considered) received by this population percentage. If 1 percent of the population receives 1 percent of total income, and 5 percent of the population receives 5 percent of income, and all other population percentages receive the corresponding percentages of income—there is no gap between the income and population percentages—the Gini coefficient would then be 0. If, at the other fanciful extreme, all income were received by a single recipient, the Gini coefficient would reach its peak—all income garnered by a single recipient—and the Gini coefficient would then be 1. The contrast at these extreme points is between "all for all" and "all for one." A Gini coefficient magnitude of .5 indicates medium inequality.

Clearly, both Gini coefficient extremes—maximum equality and maximum inequality—are "bads." However, whether any specific level or specific change in the Gini coefficient, either closer to or farther from equality, is "good" or "bad" cannot be inferred from the Gini coefficient number alone. This crucial inference depends on what accounts for the Gini coefficient inequality number. Is it because of greater work effort, higher labor productivity, innovation, entrepreneurship, better technology, or more efficient management or instead because of favoritism, nepotism, collusion, bribery, fraud, insider trading, special privilege, or other forms of corruption? If the explanation lies in higher productivity and better management, then the inequality warrants encouragement. If, instead, inequality is a result of nepotism and corruption, it should be combated and reversed.

If the answer is neither black nor white but a shade of gray, which of the explanations predominates? And how can the positive factors be encouraged while the latter are reduced?

According to the best current US government data showing Gini coefficient estimates around the world, both China and the United States are in the middle part of the Gini coefficient range (between .45 and .49). Actually, inequality in China is probably higher than this estimate and higher than in the United States—an inference I draw from a recent statement by the director of China's National Bureau of Statistics that the bureau is unable to publish Gini coefficient estimates because "data on high-income groups is incomplete."[1]

In global Gini coefficient comparisons, the pattern of inequality is decidedly mixed. European countries show less inequality than the United States. Several rapidly growing developing economies, including Brazil, show greater inequality than the United States, and a number of other countries—including Japan, South Korea, India, Turkey, and Israel—show less inequality.

This mixed picture reinforces the basic takeaway point: it is more important to know the underlying explanations for inequality across countries and within them rather than the amount of inequality or changes in it. The inequality debate should focus more on the sources and reasons for inequality and less on how much inequality there is or how much it has changed, more on explaining inequality and less on deploring it.

This is what the debate should be about but isn't.

Note

1. Fang Xuyan and Lea Yu, "Gov't Refuses to Release Gini Coefficient," *Caixin Online,* January 18, 2012, http://english.caixin.com/2012-01-18 /100349814.html.

POSTAUDIT

This essay still seems on target, although two important considerations that are missing from it would warrant attention to be updated: (1) recognition of the differences between pretax and post-tax income in China and the United States (much greater in the United States) and (2) inequality of wealth, as distinct from income. *Score: Medium*

25 A Few Low Notes Won't Spoil China-US Harmony

US-China relations, and the respective national interests that underlie them, are generally harmonious. However, this is occasionally jarred by sharp discord. At present, the discord arises from legislation pending in the US Congress to put pressure on China to substantially raise the value of its "misaligned" yuan, relative to the US dollar.

Washington's aim is to reduce the mainland's large current account surplus with the United States (nearly $200 billion last year), which, it is contended, is appreciably affected by Beijing's deliberate policy of undervaluing the yuan.

The internal American politics behind this measure is complex, and in any event, its economic logic is basically flawed.

The source of China's global surplus—and its surplus with the United States—lies in an excess of domestic savings (about 40 percent of its approximately $5 trillion gross domestic product) over its domestic investment rate (about 35 percent of gross domestic product). The American economy is characterized by a precisely opposite imbalance: an excess of gross domestic investment over domestic savings.

This article was previously published as Charles Wolf Jr., "A Few Low Notes Won't Spoil China-US Harmony," *South China Morning Post,* August 2, 2007, http://www .rand.org/blog/2007/08/a-few-low-notes-wont-spoil-china-us-harmony.html.

If, and when, these basically symbiotic imbalances become unsustainable, tinkering with the yuan-dollar exchange rate will have little influence. Quite different policy changes will be required if, for example, the US savings rate is to be boosted and China's rate is to be lowered. Moreover, if these changes are to be accomplished without triggering a recession in the United States and inflation in China, the exchange rate will be the result—not the cause—of the necessary changes.

Beyond the symbiotic relationships between the two economies, the nations' national interests are in close harmony. Both have a major interest in maintaining and enlarging a free and open global trading system and in encouraging global capital markets that allow free capital flows in both directions, facilitating American investment in China and vice versa.

As the world's first- and second-largest importers of oil, the United States and China have convergent interests in increased and diversified sources of supply and moderate and relatively stable oil prices. Both also share a strong interest in developing efficient alternatives to fossil fuels.

Energy represents a divergent, as well as a convergent, interest. The more hydrocarbon fuels each consumes, the more global oil prices will tend to rise, to the detriment of other consumers. China's subsidies to households and state enterprises thus harm US energy consumers.

Both nations have vital interests in nonproliferation of nuclear and other weapons of mass destruction. North Korea's nuclear test last October concerned China no less than the United States. But Beijing is less inclined to confront nonproliferation in Iran, as that country is a major source of China's oil imports and a growing market for its exports.

The threat of Islamic terrorism and the importance of combating it are of as deep concern to Beijing as they are to Washington, and this impels them to share intelligence, track and interdict financial transactions that may support terrorism, and cooperate in other ways.

To be sure, there are other security issues that China and the United States see in a different light. They include China's increasing military spending, the preferential treatment given by the United States to India's nuclear development, and the Taiwan issue.

In China and America's major international concerns, harmony predominates. That there are, nevertheless, important factors on both sides of the coin brings to mind an observation by F. Scott Fitzgerald about the criterion of a first-rate mind: "the ability to hold two opposed ideas in the mind at the same time, and still retain the ability to function."[1]

Whether the minds behind the respective policies in the United States and China measure up to this exacting test is an open question.

Note

1. F. Scott Fitzgerald, "The Crack-Up," *Esquire,* February 26, 2008, http://www.esquire.com/features/the-crack-up.

POSTAUDIT

Current data have obviously changed substantially: for example, China's trade and current account surpluses have halved since this piece was written in 2007. But the basic economic interdependence between the two countries remains as described in the op-ed, as do the multiplicity of other convergent and divergent interests between them—perhaps a few more of the latter than the former. *Score: Medium*

26 Bipartisanship Doesn't Help Fix Exchange Rates

Protracted partisan wrangling in recent years between Republicans and Democrats has led to national polls' ratings of congressional performance that are more than 50 percent lower than the ratings of presidential performance. The wrangling has also led to an accompanying belief that bipartisanship would result in improved public policy. Unfortunately, this belief is unwarranted: bipartisanship is not a guarantor of good policy—a point strikingly demonstrated by a major bipartisan proposal now in an advanced stage of legislative consideration in Washington to force China to revalue its currency.

Pending congressional legislation would punish China for its "misaligned" currency (the yuan). The legislation is both thoroughly bipartisan and badly flawed. Its sterling bipartisan credentials include strong support from the Democratic chairmen and ranking Republican members of the cognizant committees in both the Senate and the House. Exposing the legislation's flaws requires some further background.

China's current account surplus—the excess of its total revenues from exports of goods and services, from holdings of foreign assets, and from foreign remittances above its payments for corresponding transactions—has been sharply rising since 2000.

In 2007 China's global current account surplus will be about $300 billion, two-thirds of which represent its bilateral surplus with the United States. China's global current account surplus is about 10 percent of its gross domestic product (GDP).

Over the same period, the global current account deficit of the United States has been steadily rising. In 2007, the US deficit will be about $800 billion, nearly 6 percent of US GDP. China's bilateral current account surplus with the United States is thus one-quarter the global US deficit. The remainder of the US deficit is directly or indirectly responsible for the surpluses of the four other (apart from China) principal surplus countries: Japan, Germany, Saudi Arabia, and Russia.

Since 2005, when China began to allow the yuan's peg to the US dollar to float over a narrow band, the yuan has appreciated by 10 percent on foreign exchange markets: in 2005, the yuan was worth twelve US cents; it is currently worth slightly more than thirteen cents.

In both houses of Congress several of the most senior and influential members in both parties are convinced that the imbalanced international transactions between China and the United States are caused by China's maintenance (or "manipulation") of its "misaligned" currency. If the misalignment were corrected, they reason, by an increase in the yuan's exchange value to perhaps seventeen or eighteen cents, the bilateral imbalance would be substantially reduced if not eliminated. The reasoning is that China's exports to the United States would become more expensive in US dollars and would therefore decrease, while China's imports from the United States would become less expensive in Chinese yuan and therefore would increase. If China fails to make this adjustment, the pending legislation in Congress would impose a tax on imports from China to account for the putative undervaluation.

While this reasoning appears plausible, and while it has thoroughly persuaded the congressional leadership of both parties, it is nonetheless fundamentally wrong!

A country's global current account deficit depends on and is defined by the excess of its gross domestic investment above its gross domestic savings. In the US economy, gross savings are 10–12 percent of GDP; household and government savings from current income are slightly negative, while savings accrue largely through corporate depreciation allowances and retained corporate earnings. On the other hand, gross domestic investment is 16–17 percent of GDP. The difference between the two—gross investment and gross savings—is made up by the excess of imports over exports, thus constituting the US current account deficit.

China's current account surplus is the mirror image of the US imbalance. Although gross investment in China is high in absolute terms (above 30 percent of its GDP), its savings are still higher (above 40 percent of GDP). Appreciation of the yuan to seventeen or eighteen cents might initially raise US exports to China and lower China's exports to the United States.

However, these effects would be small and transitory as long as the fundamental imbalances between savings and investment in the two economies persist! Recent experience of Japan and Germany—two countries with perennial current account surpluses—illustrate the point.

Although Japan's yen has appreciated against the dollar in the past several years, its current account surplus remains the same because Japan's domestic savings have continued to exceed domestic investment as much as before appreciation. Among eurozone countries, Germany has maintained its large global current account surplus at the same time as the euro has appreciated by 30 percent relative to the dollar and as most other countries in the eurozone have continued to incur current account deficits.

The difference within the eurozone is explained by the fact that the German economy maintains an excess of savings over investment, while the economies of most other eurozone countries show a savings shortfall. In both Germany and Japan, the excess of domestic savings over domestic investment persists, notwithstanding currency appreciation.

To reduce the bilateral imbalances between China and the United States without triggering inflation in the former and recession in the latter requires very different and more carefully crafted policies than revaluation of the yuan. If remedies are sought in inappropriate ways, the results are likely to be perverse. For example, if correcting China's imbalance were sought by increasing gross investment, rampant inflation above the present 6 percent annual rate (already twice that of a year ago) could result, and if correcting the US imbalance were sought by lowering investment to a level closer to the low US current savings rate, a serious recession would likely result.

Effective remedial policies for China lie in raising domestic consumption by 4 or 5 percent of GDP through such measures as wider dissemination of credit and debit cards, expansion of consumer credit instruments, and improved credit ratings for consumers and for institutions that provide consumer credit. Remedial policies for the United States lie in raising current savings by 2 or 3 percent of US GDP through curbing government spending, instituting personal retirement accounts to supplement the defined benefits of Social Security, establishing a graduated consumption tax, or some combination of these measures.

In the United States, such measures have indeed been advocated by some members of both parties. But more important than their potential bipartisan support, they warrant *non*partisan support because, unlike currency realignment, they would actually address the underlying sources of the US and Chinese imbalances.

POSTAUDIT

As this October 2007 essay notes, that consensus between Democrats and Republicans is all too rare doesn't imply that, when achieved, the result will be sensible policy. The consensus that presumes China's yuan is undervalued relative to the US dollar is a case in point: consensus implies neither validity nor sensible policy. *Score: Good*

PART IV

Japan, Korea, India

27 The Asian Century

Reality or Hype?

For some time, conventional wisdom has argued that the twenty-first century will be dominated by Asia while America's global importance declines.

The narrative is this: Asian GDP will soon grow to more than 50 percent of global GDP, while America's percentage will slip to perhaps less than 15 percent. The new Asian century will therefore entail a dramatic global power shift. Even if economies such as China slow, their growth will still overwhelm the rest of the world.

Yet some strategists argue that this narrative is faulty. Clyde Prestowitz of the Economic Strategy Institute argues that the notion of "Asian GDP" makes no sense given the region's lack of unity and commonality. While it is true that the combination of India, China, and Japan yields a total GDP that is a major percentage of the global economy, this is a "meaningless combination." These countries are unlikely to be allies even in a loose sense. Besides, the United States, the European Union, Canada, Mexico, and South America already comprise more than 50 percent of global GDP. These economies are not going away.

This excerpt was previously published in "The Asian Century: Reality or Hype? Thirty-Five Experts Offer Their Predictions," *International Economy*, Summer 2013, 25–26.

Prestowitz concludes that the pan-Asian century narrative is mostly "journalistic hype." Look at today's Asian-dominated global supply chain. Supplies primarily still go to US and EU markets.

Yet others counter that the Asian economies enjoy benefits that are sure to expand. China is graduating at least three times as many science and engineering students as the United States, and India twice as many. Chinese outbound direct investment—particularly in mining, energy, and agriculture—is on the upswing.

Are we living in the second decade of an Asian century?

Both narratives are wrong, because each is misleadingly simplistic. The pessimistic narrative is wrong because the US economy will likely grow more rapidly than the economies of some other important regions and countries (such as the European Union, the Middle East, and Russia), although growing more slowly than some other important countries and regions (such as China, India, and Southeast Asia). And the US energy sector in particular is likely to expand relative to that of the rest of the world or any particular major country. Furthermore, if and when US gross domestic product reaches and sustains a more normal rate following recovery from a deep recession (say, a growth rate of 4 percent or better) by learning from the mistakes of its anemic recovery thus far, it will be growing more rapidly than the global economy as a whole.

The optimistic narrative is partly right but no less wrong on other counts. It's surely right in asserting that the India-China-Japan triad is fraught with contradictions and hence sums to a "meaningless combination." For example, Japan's and India's expanded contributions to what should more accurately be characterized as the "Asian-component" of the (rather than the "Asian-dominated") global supply chain are likely to be at the expense of China's access to US and European Union markets rather than additions to them. Recall that import demand is highly income-elastic, so supply chains will be stunted by slow growth. Nevertheless, the optimists are mistaken to take comfort from or be complacent about these prospects. There are likely to be few major international policy problems—whether economic, political, or security—to which the United States has the exclusive or even dominant answers. Mindful of US resource constraints at home and the enormously expanded, interconnected pool of energized actors throughout the world, resolution or even mitigation of these problems will entail multiple participants. Whether and how the United States can or should play a constructive yet constrained role as primus inter pares is a big, open question.

Although there's conventional wisdom on each side of the narrative, it's worth noting that there are two kinds of conventional wisdom: the kind that's presumed to be wise because it's conventional and the kind that's become conventional because it's genuinely wise. Both sides of the narrative are well represented by the former.

POSTAUDIT

Although this comment suffers from brevity (reflecting the constraints on length—three hundred words—imposed by the organizers of the symposium), the balance struck between "reality" (some) and "hype" (excessive) seems about right. *Score: Good*

28 Japan's Sun May Be Rising

A Different Cure for Economic Stagnation

Whether by design or inadvertence, Prime Minister Shinzo Abe's plans for reviving Japan's economy after two decades of stagnation differ sharply from the stimulus and austerity policies pursued by the United States and the European Union to recover from the deep recession of 2008–2009. These differences augur well for Japan's prospects.

"Abenomics" is metaphorically depicted as a quiver of "three arrows." The first is monetary policy; the second, fiscal policy; and the third—"creating wealth through growth"—is structural and reformist in character although less clearly specified than the other two.[1]

It's worth noting that it shares a few elements with the US experience and one element with EU practice. Abenomics' first arrow, aggressively easy monetary policies by the Bank of Japan, uses the same terminology—quantitative easing (QE)—adopted by the Federal Reserve during the past several years. Japan's QE is a simulacrum of QE in the United States.

Japan's QE is moving rapidly to double the economy's monetary base by 2014. By way of comparison, the Federal Reserve's QE

This article was previously published as Charles Wolf Jr., "Japan's Sun May Be Rising: A Different Cure for Economic Stagnation," *Weekly Standard*, August 19, 2013, http://www.weeklystandard.com/articles/japan-s-sun-may-be-rising_745842 .html.

boosted the US monetary base by 40 percent between 2008 and mid-2013. In both countries, monetary policy aims at maintaining near-zero interest rates, although relaxation of this target is more likely in the United States than in Japan. And unlike the Fed's version, a declared objective of Japan's QE is to raise the yen-dollar exchange rate (that is, to depreciate Japan's currency) to a target rate between 100 and 110 and thereby to stimulate Japanese exports. At the start of Abe's tenure last December, the yen-dollar rate was 87; currently, it is 99.

Abenomics' second arrow—fiscal policy—can also be compared with stimulus policies in the United States and has one element in common with austerity policies in the European Union. Like US fiscal policy, Japan's counterpart entails continued and large debt-financed government spending. The ratio of Japan's general government debt to gross domestic product (GDP) was 214 percent when Abe became prime minister—by far the highest ratio among the world's developed economies and about twice that of the United States. However, less than 10 percent of Japan's total debt is owed to foreign entities, while about one-third of US debt is held by foreign creditors (mainly China and to a lesser extent Japan). Abe's fiscal policy has raised the already-high ratio of government debt to GDP to 224 percent to stimulate demand and offset the chronic deflation plaguing Japan's economy in the past two decades.

To help finance this large-scale debt, Abenomics' fiscal policy includes a page from the European Union's austerity playbook: an added consumption tax intended to boost government revenues by 5 percent—the only instance in which Japanese and EU policies overlap.

While there are thus a few similarities between Japan's current path and the efforts of the European Union and the United States, the similarities are dwarfed by differences both qualitative and quantitative.

The qualitative differences were evident in a recent meeting between a visiting US economist and spokespersons of the Japanese cabinet secretariat, the Bank of Japan, and the Ministry of Finance. The meeting opened with an explicit statement that the new policies are intended to be "pro-business as well as pro-growth"—an eminently reasonable approach in an economy whose private sector accounts for approximately 80 percent of GDP. In the profusion of economic policy debates in the United States and European Union, such a clear and sensible declaration of intent is rarely, if ever, encountered.

The content and intent of Abenomics' third arrow displays the sharpest differences from US and EU precedents. While acknowledging the central role of Japan's world-class brands in such industries as automobiles, electronics, earth-moving equipment, and robotics, the third arrow aims at a more open, competitive Japanese economy: allowing freedom of entry for start-ups, welcoming and nurturing a more aggressive venture-capital industry, and encouraging entrepreneurship and innovation. The relative scarcity of these qualities in Japan's economy was acknowledged by the spokespersons and is evidenced by the tenfold difference between annual new start-ups in the United States and Japan (though US GDP is only about three times that of Japan's).

Although Abe proposes legislation, funding, and regulatory action to advance these aims, a gap exists between means and ends. That said, the third arrow represents a striking contrast between the path Japan is taking and that followed in the United States and European Union. One token of intent is Abenomics' proposed ten-point reduction in Japan's corporate tax rate, currently the highest among the advanced economies. The US corporate rate (35 percent) would then have that distinction, while Japan's rate would drop to 28 percent—incidentally, China's is 25 percent.

Although the three arrows are the core of Abenomics, there is another dimension that, while formally unrelated, may indirectly affect it. This dimension is Abe's declared aim of making Japan's military establishment "more normal"—that is, similar to the military establishments of other countries—by relaxing the unique restrictions imposed on Japan's self-defense forces by Article 5 of its constitution. Whether and how this issue is resolved, Japan's defense budget is likely to experience a slight increase. In past years, the defense budget has hovered slightly below 1 percent of GDP. Henceforth, it is likely to hover slightly above that threshold. This increase in spending and procurement will, of course, be only a small part of the fiscal stimulus embodied in the second arrow of Abenomics. As the increase occurs, however, Japan will be unique among America's major allies in increasing its defense budget, although as a share of GDP the Japanese figure will still be relatively low.

What are the chances that Abe's efforts will succeed in reviving Japan's economy from its torpor? In many ways, the obstacles facing Japan are even greater than those faced by the United States and European Union. Japan's zero-growth stagnation has lasted much longer (since 1990) than the subprime crisis afflicting the United States and European Union, to which Japan was much less exposed. Japan's protracted stagnation spawned chronic deflation, thereby imposing unique disincentives to consume or invest: when future prices are expected to decline, current spending tends to be postponed.

Japan's revival is further impeded by acutely unfavorable demographics: a declining and aging population and a rising dependency ratio of the elderly to the working-age labor force. Mitigating these conditions will require measures beyond Abenomics. Japan's difficulties have been aggravated by the tsunami and nuclear disasters of 2011. And the ability of Japan's world-class companies to uplift and drive the economy has been eroded by aggressive competitors in the United States, Korea, Germany, and China.

Yet Japan also has significant advantages in responding to these challenges. Abe's political position has been strengthened and secured for at least three more years by the Liberal Democratic Party's dominance in both the upper and lower houses of Japan's Diet. Furthermore, his ability to implement the three-arrows program is less constrained by special interests, lobbies, and labor (company unions are prevalent in Japan rather than the national trade unions of the West). While business leaders profess strong support for Abenomics—especially some of its tax and structural reforms—their plans eschew any reliance on government subsidies or bailouts. The Nikkei's rise of 32 percent since Abe became prime minister in December is a bellwether of Japan's collective expectations about the economy.

If and as these expectations become reality—including evidence of military "normalcy"—Japan's prominence in the global arena will be enhanced. The sun that has been setting may rise again. Still, a realistically optimistic assessment of the chance of success is likely to hover slightly above fifty-fifty.

Note

1. Cabinet Secretary of Japan, briefing to the author, July 2013, Tokyo.

POSTAUDIT

The effectiveness of Shinzo Abe's economic policies remains uncertain. Abenomics focuses explicitly on the private, market-based sector and on a combination of austerity and stimulus measures to encourage it. The package warrants at least the modest degree of optimism expressed in this essay, although the short interval since it was written precludes any claim for prescience. *Score: Good*

29 China and India, 2025

A Macroeconomic Assessment

CHARLES WOLF JR. AND
ALISHER AKHMEDJONOV

Two centuries ago, Edmund Burke advised a British parliamentarian, "Never plan the future by the past." A century later Winston Churchill cautioned, "If we open a quarrel between the past and the present, we shall find that we have lost the future." These admonitions recall a more recent truism, often attributed to Yogi Berra: "It's dangerous to make predictions, especially about the future!"

The assessments described in this chapter violate these precepts by using data from the past and the present to make forecasts about the future.[1] Consequently, I should emphasize not only the uncertainties that generally and inherently surround forecasts but also and especially the uncertainties accompanying the forecasts described in this chapter because they pertain to two rapidly changing economies and polities that are affected by, as well as interacting with, rapidly changing regional and global environment.

This article was previously published as Charles Wolf Jr. and Alisher Akhmedjonov, "China and India, 2025: A Macroeconomic Assessment," in *Handbook of Emerging Economies,* ed. Robert E. Looney (Abingdon, UK: Routledge, 2014), 539–554.

Forecasts of Economic Growth in the
People's Republic of China and India

Economic growth in China and India has become the focus of increased attention in Asia, in the Asia-Pacific Economic Cooperation (APEC) forum, in the G20, and in the global economy. In recent decades, growth in both countries has exceeded expectations. China recorded an average annual growth in real gross domestic product (GDP) of 9–10 percent, while India's growth during the same period was 7–8 percent. Both countries face the challenge of sustaining such high rates of growth. This chapter summarizes a meta-analysis of growth estimates for China and India for the period from the first decade of the twenty-first century to 2025, based on twenty-seven separate studies, undertaken in three different institutional settings: universities, business, and international organizations.[2] The meta-analysis also summarizes and evaluates several of the key assumptions underlying the estimates. Finally, the chapter compares five different scenarios of high, low, and average growth estimates for the two countries and concludes with several inferences based on this analysis.

The twenty-seven studies included in the analysis were done between 2000 and 2008 and covered the two countries' recent and prospective levels and growth of GDP, capital, employment, and total factor productivity (TFP). The studies were culled from a larger set of four dozen studies, with selections based on the sufficiency and comparability of their data for the comparative assessment that was our aim. Most of the studies contained explicit projections of these macroeconomic indicators to 2025. Where estimates of the indicators were implicit, we derived the relevant values using incremental capital-output ratios, or Cobb-Douglas production functions, or a combination of both methods. The detailed steps of this meta-analysis are described in the appendix to this chapter.

The analytic methods used in the underlying studies vary widely. Some rely on simple extrapolation and trend analysis in forecasting growth of GDP and its components, while other studies use more sophisticated models. Some analyses concentrate on a single aspect of economic growth—for example, the role of capital accumulation and its determinants in explaining differences between the two economies—while other studies consider other factors such as demographics, labor markets, and education, as well as trade and fiscal policies affecting growth. Some of the studies provide forecasts only to 2020, while others extend to 2050. A few of the studies focus more on either China or India rather than giving equal attention to both countries. In these few cases, we supplemented some details that were implicit in a particular study to provide comparable results using similar methods and data for both countries.

Our review of forecasted GDP growth rates in the pooled studies of China and India to 2025 suggests that the recent rapid growth of these countries is only likely to be sustainable in the future at a slower pace. As shown in Table 29.1 and Figure 29.1, for the pooled studies, average and GDP growth rates are projected to be 5.7 percent in China and 5.6 percent in India between 2020 and 2025. During the same period, the average annual estimates of growth in the accumulated stock of capital are 6.1 percent for China and 6.9 percent for India; for growth in employment, the average estimates are 0.4 percent for China and 1.6 percent for India; and for growth in TFP, the average estimates are 3.4 percent for China and 2.1 percent for India.

These estimates of average rates are, unsurprisingly, accompanied by major uncertainties, as suggested by the wide range between the highest and lowest growth estimates and their corresponding variances.[3] In the twenty-seven studies we selected, the estimates for GDP growth rates for the 2020–2025 period range from 3.8 to 9.0 percent for China and from 2.8 to 8.4 percent for India. For the growth rates in capital stock, estimates range from

Table 29.1   China-India macroeconomic meta-analysis:
summary of salient estimates, 2020–2025

	GDP		TFP		EMPLOYMENT		CAPITAL	
	China	*India*	*China*	*India*	*China*	*India*	*China*	*India*
Mean	5.7	5.6	3.4	2.1	0.4	1.6	6.1	6.9
Max	9.0	8.4	5.6	3.6	0.6	1.9	9.4	9.8
Min	3.8	2.8	2.1	0.1	−0.1	0.7	4.2	3.9
Variance	2.2	2.3	1.0	1.0	0.0	0.1	2.1	2.5
n (obser-vations)	28	26	28	26	28	26	28	26
n (studies)				27				

Note: Growth rates are given in percentage per year. The number of observations does not match the total number of studies because some studies provide estimates for either China or India but not both. GDP = gross domestic product; TFP = total factor productivity.

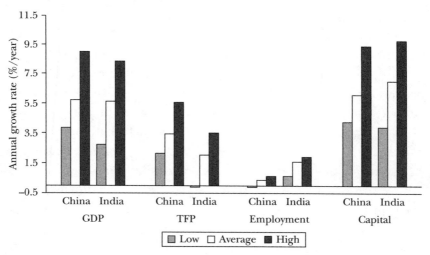

Figure 29.1   China-India macroeconomic comparisons: salient estimates, 2020–2025

4.2 to 9.4 percent for China and from 3.9 to 9.8 percent for India. For employment growth rates, the range is from −0.1 to 0.6 percent for China and from 0.7 to 1.9 percent for India. For TFP, the estimated growth rates range from 2.1 to 5.6 percent for China and from 0.1 to 3.6 percent for India.[4]

In the following section, we review these estimates by separating them into three clusters: (1) those by academic authors and institutions, (2) those by business organizations and authors (e.g., Goldman Sachs, PricewaterhouseCoopers, McKinsey), and (3) those by international organizations (e.g., the World Bank, the International Monetary Fund). We also evaluate the differing assumptions that may contribute to the wide range of the estimates and highlight several other contrasting aspects of the three clusters.

Studies by Academic Authors and Institutions

Of the studies in the meta-analysis, eleven are by university-based academic authors.[5] Interestingly, the academic cluster generates the widest ranges of growth estimates for China and India as summarized in Table 29.2. Within this cluster, the highest estimate for China's annual GDP growth for 2020–2025 is 9 percent and the lowest is 3.8 percent. For India, the estimates for annual GDP growth within this cluster range from 7.2 to 2.8 percent. Again, the variances of estimates in this group are higher than for the

Table 29.2   China-India GDP growth
estimates by academic authors,
2020–2025 (%/year)

	China	India
Low	3.8	2.8
High	9.0	7.2
Average	5.5	4.3
Variance	2.6	2.4
n (observations)	15	9
n (studies)	11	7

Note: Differences between the numbers of observations and of studies arise because several studies included both high- and low-growth forecasts by their authors.

studies by business groups and international organizations. That the variance in the academic authors' estimates is by far the largest among the three clusters will be surprising to some but unsurprising to others. Later in this chapter we suggest some hypotheses—more accurately, some conjectures—to account for the variances.

In making these estimates, the academic authors tend to focus especially on one or two aspects of each country's growth. For example, some studies in this cluster focus on demographic changes in China and India (Golley and Tyers 2006; Tyers, Golley, and Bain 2006). Another forecast in this cluster focuses on the two countries' roles in global energy markets, their greenhouse gas emissions, and the presumed effects on growth (Paltsev and Reilly 2007a). Still another study in this cluster focuses on China's regional economic structure, basing its estimates on sectoral and regional economic growth (Huang et al. 2003). Several studies base their long-term forecasts on a standard Cobb-Douglas production function (Holz 2005; Poncet 2006).

Carsten Holz (2005), from the Hong Kong University of Science and Technology, projects the highest annual GDP growth rate for China (9 percent) for the 2020–2025 period, arguing that China can expect many years of rapid economic growth. Holz's forecast mainly rests on projecting recent growth rates into the future; he concludes that China's GDP will surpass that of the United States in purchasing power terms by the middle of the next decade.[6] He suggests this trajectory will follow the examples of Japan, Taiwan, and the Republic of Korea (South Korea) in the early stages of their development. Holz contends that the structural changes taking place in China, along with factor price equalizations, will match the patterns of growth achieved by these other Asian countries.

In sharp contrast, another author in the academic cluster (Laurent 2006) suggests that China's average annual GDP growth rate in 2020–2025 will decline to 3.8 percent, reasoning that declining numbers of prime working-age workers will inhibit China's growth. Clint Laurent contends that India's growing labor force might enable India to grow more rapidly if its populace were more highly educated. However, unlike other economists who compare the two economies, Laurent is pessimistic about India's ability to educate its population. He expresses little confidence that this will happen and forecasts that India's average annual GDP growth in 2020–2025 will fall to 3.4 percent.

The effect of declining population on economic growth is also among the most significant issues raised in the study by Rod Tyers, Jane Golley, and Iain Bain (2006), from the Australian National University (ANU). Their study suggests that relative labor abundance in India will bring higher capital returns and attract a rising share of global foreign direct investment to India.[7] Accordingly, their forecast for India's annual growth rate in 2020–2025 is 7.2 percent. The authors believe that India will displace China as the world's most rapidly expanding economy.

The ANU authors also examine the economic impact of a hypothetical increase in fertility in China that might occur if (1) China were to abandon its one-child policy and (2) a more-rapid-than-expected reduction of fertility were to occur in India. The ANU authors question the plausibility of this scenario by noting that even if China were to abandon its one-child policy, fertility might not rise substantially; the authors point to the reduction in fertility in China that occurred before the introduction of the one-child policy in 1979 (Carnell 2000) to show that forces other than policy have influenced China's fertility rate. For example, fertility is sensitive to cultural norms and economic incentives. Consequently, if a norm of low fertility has indeed taken root in China, it may be difficult to reverse. In India, too, fertility has been falling slowly (see Wolf et al. 2011). An acceleration of fertility reduction in India might occur either as a consequence of economic development or because of exogenous societal reasons.

A contrasting study from scholars at the Massachusetts Institute of Technology (MIT) (Paltsev and Reilly 2007b) forecasts that India's average annual GDP growth rate in 2020–2025 may be as low as 2.8 percent, in particular because of high energy prices that would put a heavier burden on India's increasing oil imports. However, the MIT paper ignores the possible effects of new technologies that might partly reduce dependence on fossil fuel imports and lower their prices.

Similar to Holz (2005), Sandra Poncet (2006) at CEPII, a French academic research center on international economics, uses a production function based on a neoclassical model in which GDP growth depends on growth of the labor force, of capital, and of TFP. Poncet's GDP projections for both China and India are modest, placing them at average annual rates of 4.6 percent and 4.5 percent, respectively, during the period.

Unlike other studies in the three clusters of the meta-analysis, in which TFP enters the growth forecasts exogenously (Poddar and Yi 2007; Hofman and Kuijs 2008; Rodrik and Subramanian 2004) or is modeled as a process of catch-up (Wilson and Purushothaman 2003), Poncet links the growth of TFP to investment in human capital. Growth in TFP becomes an endogenous function of average years of education and the income gap compared with income in the United States. The resulting differences in TFP and in the growth projections for India and China are thereby enlarged. Taking into account expected improvements in education, Poncet projects the average annual growth of TFP in 2020–2025 as 2.5 percent in China and 1.9 percent in India. In particular, Poncet projects that China's and India's GDPs could grow at yearly average rates of 4.6 percent and 4.5 percent, respectively, during the period.

One paper in the academic cluster (Hofman and Kuijs 2008) estimates an average annual GDP growth rate for China of 6.7 percent during 2020–2025 while suggesting that China's recent 9 percent growth rate is unlikely to be sustainable. The authors believe that the greatest threat to China's future growth lies in the internal imbalance between aggregate domestic savings and domestic investment that has developed since 2005. They estimate that China's aggregate national savings have come to exceed aggregate domestic investment by 12 percent of GDP. Some researchers have paid less attention to this imbalance, focusing instead on the external imbalances reflected in China's large and continuing current account surpluses. In fact, the two sets of imbalances are exactly equal to one another because of the basic accounting identity that defines how the external and internal flow of funds is calculated.[8]

According to Bert Hofman and Louis Kuijs (2008), China's aggregate surplus of savings is due largely to rapid increases in enterprise savings, whereas household and government savings have been stable or declining in recent years.[9] China's corporate sector has been enjoying high profits, while the wage share of GDP has been declining. The authors argue that this disparity is at the heart of China's growing income inequality, and they suggest that this is further exacerbated by the low returns earned by China's savers in financial markets (about 2.5 percent), despite the economy's rapid growth.

Studies by Business Organizations and Authors

We included nine studies by business organizations and authors in the pool of twenty-seven studies.[10] Table 29.3 summarizes the range of GDP growth estimates generated by this cluster. The studies in the business cluster are typically based on the neoclassical growth model referred to above, and they generate a relatively narrow range of annual GPD growth estimates for China from 2020 to 2025: between 4.5 and 5.2 percent. In contrast, the range of growth estimates for India is considerably wider:

Table 29.3 China-India GDP growth
estimates by business organizations
and authors, 2020–2025 (%/year)

	China	India
Low	4.5	5.4
High	5.2	8.4
Average	4.7	6.3
Variance	0.1	1.1
n (observations)	6	9
n (studies)	6	9

between 5.4 and 8.4 percent. The 8.4 percent estimate is from a Goldman Sachs paper (Wilson and Purushothaman 2003) that optimistically posits high productivity growth, generally favorable demographic conditions, and improvements in educational attainment.

In contrast to the average growth estimates of the academic cluster, the business cluster places India's expected GDP growth rates in 2020–2025 *above China*'s—specifically, an average estimate of annual GDP growth of 6.3 percent for India versus 4.7 percent for China. These figures contrast with the academic cluster's average estimate of 5.4 percent for China and 4.3 percent for India, cited earlier. Furthermore, the variance estimates for the business cluster are substantially lower than for the academic cluster.

Not surprisingly, the papers in the business cluster, especially those sponsored by Goldman Sachs, accord particular importance to the prevailing regulatory environment and the protection of property rights in influencing their growth forecasts. This emphasis is missing in the papers by the academic institutions discussed earlier and in the international organizations studies discussed later.

The studies sponsored by the business organizations also tend to compare their estimates for China and India with those of other Asian economics—in particular, South Korea—a characteristic that the business cluster shares with the cluster of studies by international financial instructions.

The study sponsored by Goldman Sachs (Wilson and Purushothaman 2003) suggests that if certain conditions prevail in China—macroeconomic stability, high investment rates, and a large labor force—the result will likely make China the world's largest economy by 2041, when China's per capita income is estimated to be $30,000.[11] According to this study, India's growth rate is likely to remain above 5 percent for several decades, and its GDP will exceed Japan's by 2032, reaching a level of per capita income thirty-five times its current level yet still significantly lower than China's in 2050.

Wilson and Purushothaman make several simplifying assumptions that indeed cast doubt on their final estimates. For example, they do not consider changing demographic conditions in China, instead making the erroneous assumption that the proportion of the working-age population in China will remain stable. In reality, the percentage of China's working-age population is expected to peak in 2010–2012 and to decline thereafter (Wolf et al. 2011). Furthermore, Wilson and Purushothaman make an unrealistic assumption that the investment rate of economies seeking to catch up with the developed countries will remain very high and constant. It is more realistic to assume that as India's and China's per capita income levels approach those of the developed countries, they will experience lower rates of return on investment and therefore will reduce their rates of investment, leading to lower rates of growth in TFP. These reduced rates will tend to converge more closely with those prevailing in more advanced economies. For example, developing countries that previously maintained an investment rate of 25–30 percent of GDP are likely to find these rates converging toward prevailing levels in Organisation for Economic Co-operation and Development (OECD) countries (about 15–20 percent),[12] because of the lower rates of return on new investment.

A sequel Goldman Sachs paper (Purushothaman 2004) places India's annual GDP growth at about 5.7 percent during 2020–2025, reasoning that the two crucial conditions of improved infrastructure and expanded education may be insufficient to keep India on a steady and higher growth path. Another Goldman Sachs paper (Poddar and Yi 2007) calls attention to certain constraints on doing business in India as potential threats to private enterprise (see Table 29.4; see also Figure 29.4 later in the chapter).

A paper sponsored by Deutsche Bank (Bergheim 2005) projects India to grow more rapidly than China in the period from 2010 to 2020. The Stefan Bergheim paper forecasts India's average annual GDP growth at 5.5 percent, compared with projected Chinese GDP growth of 5.2 percent over the same period. The major contributor to this gap, according to Bergheim, is China's slower population growth rate (at 0.8 percent annually, about half

Table 29.4   Business conditions in China and India, 2007

	India	China	South Korea
Starting a business			
Time required (months)	1.1	1.2	0.6
Cost (% of GDP per capita)	74.6	8.4	16.9
Contract enforcement			
Procedures required	46	35	35
Time (months)	47.3	13.5	7.7
Property registration			
Procedures required	6	4	7
Time (months)	2.1	1	0.4
Closing a business			
Recovery rate (cents on the dollar)	11.6	35.8	81.2
Time (months)	120	20.4	18

Source: Based on data from World Bank 2007.

that of India's growth rate), a presumed consequence of its one-child policy.

Analysts from the McKinsey Global Institute (Ablett et al. 2007) suggest that India's likely continuation of its recent rapid growth will result in the tripling of India's average household income over the next two decades. If this trend is sustained, India will become the world's fifth-largest economy by 2025, compared with its current position of twelfth largest. Unlike other studies in the business organization cluster, and while noting the progress that India has made to date, the McKinsey paper emphasizes the significant challenges it still faces. These include, for example, the large regional disparities in growth and poverty levels: for example, India's southern and western states prosper, while the northern and eastern states lag far behind. Furthermore, while India has been slowly urbanizing over the past two decades, the McKinsey study suggests that it remains the least urbanized of the emerging Asian economies. According to the study's analysts, only 29 percent of the Indian population currently lives in cities, compared with 40 percent in China and 48 percent in Indonesia. The McKinsey analysts project that the level of urbanization will increase to only 37 percent by 2025 in India. Finally, they note that while more Indians are completing secondary and higher education, India's education system remains severely strained and that opportunities for schooling vary widely, as does the quality of schooling. Indeed, nearly all of the business group authors stress educational inequality in India as a significant impediment and a relative disadvantage in comparison with the educational conditions in China.[13]

Studies by International Organizations

We included seven studies by international organizations in the pooled set.[14] Table 29.5 summarizes the international organizations' GDP growth estimates for China and India in 2020–2025. This

Table 29.5   China-India GDP growth rate estimates
by the three clusters, 2020–2025 (%/year)

	Country	Minimum	Maximum	Average	Variance
Academic	China	3.8	9.0	5.5	2.6
institutions	India	2.8	7.2	4.3	2.4
Business	China	4.5	5.2	4.7	0.1
organizations	India	5.4	8.4	6.3	1.1
International	China	5.9	9.0	6.8	1.1
organizations	India	5.2	8.0	6.2	0.9

cluster projects higher growth estimates than those made by the business cluster, but the international organizations' estimates are similar to those in the academic cluster. Whereas the business cluster's range of growth estimates is wider for India than for China, the international organization cluster shows a wider range in the estimates for China than for India, although the variance of the estimates for China is still lower than the variance in the academic cluster's estimates.

An anthology published by the World Bank (Winters and Yusuf 2007) provides several analytic models for assessing developments in the Chinese and Indian economies and their impact on global markets to 2020. In addition to providing forecasts of the two countries' economic growth, the World Bank study analyzes, to 2020, what would occur if China were to grow at an annual average rate of 6.6 percent and India at 5.5 percent. Several essays explore other facets of China's and India's growth, including effects on the geographic location of global industry, changes in the international financial system, effects on the global environment, and the relationship between growth and governments.

A paper from the International Monetary Fund (IMF) (Rodrik and Subramanian 2004) estimating India's annual GDP growth during 2020–2025 employs a growth-accounting model based on inputs of capital and labor and increases in TFP. Rodrik and Subramanian acknowledge that their estimate may be low if India succeeds in expanding and improving its educational system. They note that India's productivity growth has benefited from its stock of highly educated people, although the authors do not provide much supporting evidence. They also acknowledge that their growth forecasts rely on continuation of effective economic and social reforms in India. Rodrik and Subramanian also contend that, unlike China, India already has strong economic and political institutions, so that further reform need not be burdensome. Instead, they suggest that India "has done the really hard work of building good economic and political institutions—a stable democratic polity, reasonable rule of law, and protection of property rights," concluding that "countries with good institutions do not in general experience large declines in growth" (Rodrik and Subramanian 2004, 7–8).

As previously noted, not all the authors and clusters of studies agree with this judgment. Instead, some of the other studies contend that the effectiveness of India's institutions leaves much to be desired (e.g., Poddar and Yi 2007).

Similarities and Differences among the Clusters: Observations and Hypotheses

As indicated in Table 29.1 and the preceding sections, forecasts of the absolute and relative macroeconomic performance of India and China in 2020–2025 reflect deep and pervasive uncertainty. Estimates of China's and India's annual economic growth over this period vary by a factor greater than two (3.8–9.0 percent) for China and by a factor of three (2.8–8.4 percent) for India across the twenty-seven studies included in the analysis. The range in forecasts for the United States and most OECD countries would be much narrower.

Table 29.5 and Figure 29.2 summarize how the three clusters of our pooled studies differ from each other. For example, the widest variation in growth estimates for both China and India comes from the academic cluster. Table 29.5 also shows that the estimates of growth rates made by scholars at international organizations tend to be the highest among the three clusters, while the estimates from the business cluster show the widest difference in the growth estimates between India and China. Furthermore, the business cluster also projects distinctly higher growth estimates for India than for China.

The constraining forecasts of the three clusters are also displayed in the box diagram of Figure 29.3, in which India's annual growth is indicated along the vertical axis, China's on the horizontal axis. The three rectangles show the distribution of the summary statistics for, respectively, the business cluster, the academic cluster, and the international cluster. The means for each cluster are indicated by the shaded dots in each rectangle. The lower-growth

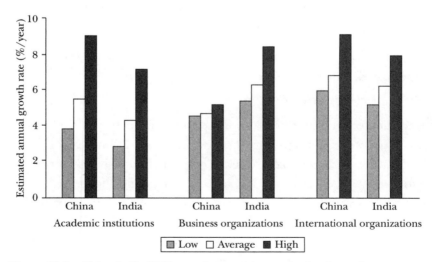

Figure 29.2   China-India GDP growth rate estimates by the three clusters, 2020–2025

estimates for India and China for each cluster are represented by
the lower-left corner of each rectangle, and the highest-growth
estimates are represented by the upper-right corner of each rectangle. The x's shown in Figure 29.3 represent, from top right to
bottom left, the high, average, and low China-India growth estimates for the pooled set of all twenty-seven studies included in the
meta-analysis.[15]

Interpreting, let alone explaining, the notable differences
among the three clusters is bound to be conjectural. For example, the widest variances characterizing the academic cluster's
estimates might plausibly be attributed to greater awareness by
the scholarly community of the enormous sources of uncertainty
affecting economic forecasts a decade and a half into the future.
Another influence contributing to this spread may lie in differences in worldviews among members of the academic community;

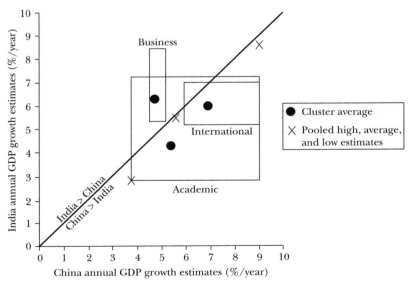

Figure 29.3   Summary of the average, high, and low estimates for all twenty-
seven studies and by cluster

for example, some academic economists are inclined to favor central planning and an expanded role of government in economic development, while others are inclined to favor greater reliance on competitive markets, market-based pricing, and decentralized innovation in determining resource allocation. Those who favor central planning may tend to see a rosier outlook for China, while those who adhere to the free-market view may be inclined to view India's prospects with greater optimism. The result of these differing dispositions and behaviors may be the widened variance of their respective forecasts within the academic cluster compared with the two other clusters.

By similar reasoning it may be presumed that studies of economic growth sponsored by business organizations might tend to be led by economists inclined toward market-based development. Hence, such studies are probably more likely to view India's democracy, rule of law, and legally protected property rights as constituting a more propitious environment for business innovation and long-term economic growth than that provided by China's one-party autocracy. Consequently, it is not surprising that the highest growth estimates for India relative to China come from the business-sponsored studies included in the meta-analysis.

Finally, that the forecasts made by the international organizations' studies show a marked advantage for China's expected growth relative to India's may plausibly be attributed to China's more prominent role in international trade and investment markets relative to India. As a consequence, one might expect international organizations to be particularly cognizant of this fact and perhaps influenced by it in their estimates of the two economies' growth over the next fifteen years, resulting in the relatively buoyant forecasts for China.

Underlying and contributing to the wide differences in forecasts are significant differences in the assumptions made by the forecasters. For example, some of the forecasts simply assume a continuation of recent growth trends in both countries, extrapolating linearly to forecast the 2020–2025 period. Other forecasts focus especially on demographic trends and especially trends in labor supplies that inhere in the current circumstances of the two countries' population cohorts and fertility rates. Still other forecasts build their estimating models on assumptions relating to energy prices and the heavy dependence of the two countries on fossil fuel imports. Further, some of the forecasts make assumptions about the prevalence of macroeconomic stability, economic openness, the quality or the degree of inequality of educational opportunities, and the integrity of economic and social institutions. Embedded in most of the studies that use the neoclassical model described earlier are simplifying and arguable assumptions about constant returns to scale and competitive markets.

In turn, these assumptions and the selectivity of their focus affect the inputs to the analytic models that the authors use in generating their respective forecasts. In the process, the forecasts ignore cyclical fluctuations around long-term trend estimates. Furthermore, the studies generally ignore the possibility of major adverse political disturbances, natural disasters, or military conflict or the possibility of a major technological jump that might trigger a new wave of innovation in China or India or that might cause a sharp change in the relative prices of the natural resources, fossil fuels, and ferrous and nonferrous metals of which China and India are major importers.

Always implicit, and sometimes explicit, in the forecasts is a recognition by the authors that China and India have taken quite different paths in pursuing economic developments. China has emphasized the expansion of labor-intensive manufacturing, while India has charted a path from agriculture to high-end service with a limited increase in the manufacturing sector. In sum, the wide range of the estimates reflects the assumptions and behavioral dispositions of the forecasters, the issues on which they focus as well as those they ignore, and the deep uncertainties that surround forecasts over the next decade and a half.

Five Growth Scenarios and Concluding Observations

The meta-analysis discussed in the preceding sections displays quantitatively the profound uncertainties that pervade attempts to forecast how two such dynamic and complex systems as the economies of India and China will fare over the next fifteen years. This uncertainty pervades the twenty-seven studies encompassed in our analysis, whether they are examined in the aggregate or within the three separate clusters of the academic, business, and international organization studies.

In this section, we contrast five scenarios consisting of different pairings of the forecasts for the two countries: a scenario in which both countries grow at their respective average estimates and scenarios that show the four combinations of the separate high- and low-growth estimates for China and India. On the implicit but not implausible premise that many of the factors affecting the economic performance of China and India (e.g., their respective fiscal and monetary policies, trade and investment policies, education policies, and business regulatory policies) are uncorrelated with one another, these starkly contrasting high-low scenarios can serve two purposes: first, to highlight (and in some sense magnify) the uncertainties that emerge from the meta-analysis and, second, to provide a basis for contingency planning for policy makers. More specifically, the challenges that US policy makers, as well as policy makers in other countries, face will be very different depending on which of the contrasting scenarios ensues. That said, it should also be noted that the most appropriate policy responses to the contrasting scenarios are more likely to involve adjusting to the scenarios rather than shaping them. However, it would be going too far to suggest that US policy is without some modest influence on which scenario occurs, although, realistically speaking, the extent of such influence, as well as of the resources that the United States is likely to be willing to deploy to affect scenario outcomes, will at most probably affect the scenarios only at their margins rather than their defining cores.

Figure 29.4 shows the five contrasting GDP growth pairings between China and India in 2020–2025 under the five contrasting scenarios.

Figures 29.5 and 29.6 show the GDPs for India and China in 2025 in terms of market exchange rate (Figure 29.5) and PPP conversion rates (Figure 29.6). As the two figures indicate, only in the scenario in which high growth in India is paired with low growth in China does India's GDP approach China's. In the four other scenarios, China's predominance is decisive. This outcome is the same whether conversions are calculated with market exchange rates or PPP rates.

Turning to a more qualitative aspect of the China-India assessment, Table 29.6 distills from the meta-analysis our judgment about the advantages and disadvantages of China and India in

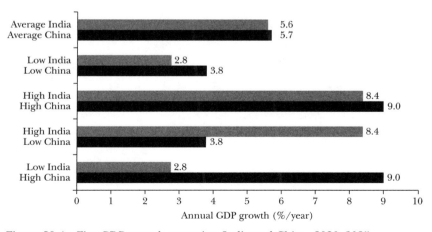

Figure 29.4   Five GDP growth scenarios, India and China, 2020–2025

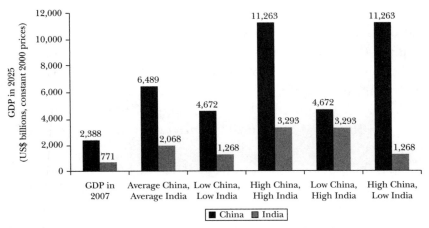

Figure 29.5   Five scenarios: GDPs of China and India in 2025, market
exchange rates
Note: Conversion to market exchange rates is based on the World Bank's World
Development Indicators.

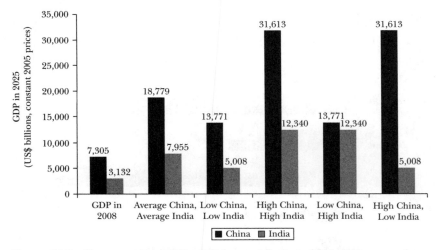

Figure 29.6   Five scenarios: GDPs of China and India in 2025, PPP conversion
rates

Table 29.6   Some qualitative factors affecting China's and India's performance

Factor	Advantage of China or India
Democracy/rule of law	India
Information technology and service skills	India
Institutions	India
Property rights	India
Productivity growth	China
Foreign investment in and by each country	China
Infrastructure	China

their respective institutional and other circumstances. Whether and to what extent the factors listed in the table will enable India to move closer to, or ahead of, China after 2025 is worthy of separate consideration beyond that provided in this chapter.

Appendix: Meta-analysis of Economic Growth in China and India

The first step in the meta-analysis involved collecting pertinent and accessible studies done between 2000 and 2008 addressing economic growth in China and India for roughly the 2010–2025 period. The major sources consulted for the search included publication indexes, LexisNexis, and Internet search engines. This search yielded an initial pool of forty-seven studies.

The second step excluded twenty studies because of incomplete or otherwise insufficient data for the two-country comparison, leaving a subset of twenty-seven studies that had the requisite data from India and China to permit their comparative assessment for 2020–2025.

The third step required drawing data from each study to make calculations of the recent and out-year rates of growth of GDP, employment, capital, and TFP, either directly from the study or indirectly using incremental capital-output ratios, or a Cobb-Douglas production function, or a growth-accounting methodology. Of the forty-seven studies, twenty-seven met these criteria for inclusion in the meta-analysis.

In the fourth step, these twenty-seven studies and the corresponding descriptive statistics on GDP and factor growth rates, means, minima, maxima, and variances were arrayed into three separate groups, or clusters, of studies as follow:

- academic authors and institutions
- business organizations (e.g., Goldman Sachs, Pricewater-houseCoopers, McKinsey)
- international financial institutions (e.g., the World Bank, the IMF, Asian Development Bank)

This step included comparisons of the descriptive statistics across the three clusters of studies, highlighting their similarities and differences.

In addition to the descriptive statistics and the comparisons across the three clusters, the text discussion of the meta-analysis includes more detailed discussion of seventeen of the twenty-seven papers included in the meta-analysis.

Figure 29.7 summarizes the successive steps.

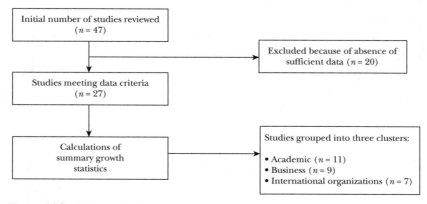

Figure 29.7   Meta-analysis process

Notes

1. This chapter draws heavily from Wolf and Akhmedjonov 2011.

2. For the list of the twenty-seven studies, see the references. For their separation into the three institutional clusters, see below.

3. We deliberately focus on the extremes of the range, rather than on maximum likelihood estimates, to highlight the uncertainties involved in these forecasts. In turn, later in this chapter we use the maximum and minimum points of the range to formulate high- and low-growth scenarios to compare Indian and Chinese GDP forecasts for 2025.

4. The corresponding variances are discussed below.

5. The eleven in the academic cluster are Brown 2005; Golley and Tyers 2006; Hofman and Kuijis 2007; Holz 2005; Huang et al. 2003; Laurent 2006; Linn 2006; Paltsev and Reilly 2007a, 2007b; Poncet 2006; and Tyers et al. 2006.

6. Holz assumes that the US average annual GDP growth rate during this period will be 3.0 percent.

7. Tyers and colleagues assume that with increasingly open capital accounts, China and India stand to attract foreign investment the more rapidly their labor forces grow.

8. The accounting identity specifies that the difference between an economy's aggregate savings and aggregate investment is equal to the difference between (1) the sum of its exports and other current international earnings and (2) its imports and other current international payments. Thus, the internal and external imbalances must be exactly equal.

9. One author of this chapter (Wolf) considers this assertion to be wrong because data from the State Statistical Bureau indicate that household savings (and household holdings of liquid savings balances in the major state banks) have grown substantially in recent years.

10. The nine studies in the business cluster are Ablett et al. 2007; Bergheim 2005; Desai et al. 2007; Hawksworth and Cookson 2008; O'Neill et al. 2005; Poddar and Yi 2007; Purushothaman 2004; Wilson and Purushothaman 2003; and Wilson and Stupnytska 2007.

11. Dominic Wilson and Roopa Purushothaman (2003) assume that the US annual GDP growth rate during the same period is between 2.1 percent and 3.1 percent. Per capita income levels are in market

exchange rates but closer to purchasing power parity (PPP) exchange rates. Wilson and Purushothaman assume that as countries develop, there will be a tendency for their currencies to converge toward PPP rates. PPP exchange rates are calculated as the ratio between a market basket of goods and services (e.g., consisting of consumer purchases or the country's GDP as a whole), priced according to the country's own prices and weighted by their corresponding shares, divided by the same weighted market basket of goods and services but instead prices in prevailing US dollar prices. Hence, PPP rates omit the effects of capital transaction, which heavily influence market exchange rates, while market exchange rates omit the effects of nontradable goods and services (e.g., residential property values and domestic household services). In developing countries, PPP exchange rates are predictably higher for domestic currencies (e.g., Indian rupees and Chinese renminbi) than are their market exchange rates.

12. See the World Bank and OECD statistical yearbooks for 2010 and 2011.

13. Heng Quan (2008) has observed Gini coefficients (reflecting socioeconomic inequality) for both China and India since 1980. He shows that China's regional differences were higher than those of India before 1990–1991, reflected in India's lower Gini coefficient. However, India's coefficient has increased since 1991, evidently exceeding that of China.

14. The seven studies in the international organization cluster are Cooper 2005; Das Gupta et al. 2003; Rodrik and Subramanian 2004; Shiyang 2007; US Department of Energy, Energy Information Administration 2008; Winters and Yusuf 2007; and World Economic Forum 2006.

15. We are indebted to RAND colleague Michael Mattrock for this graphic.

References

Ablett, Jonathan, Aardarsh Baijal, Eric Beinhocker, Anupam Bose, Diana Farrell, Ulrich Gersch, Ezra Greenberg, Shishir Gupta, and

Sumit Gupta. 2007. *The "Bird of Gold": The Rise of India's Consumer Market.* Mumbai: McKinsey Global Institute.

Bergheim, Stefan. 2005. "Global Growth Centres 2020: *Formel-G* for 34 Economies." Deutsche Bank Research *Current Issues* (March 23).

Brown, Harold. 2005. "Managing Change: China and the United States in 2025." Paper presented at the Eighth Annual RAND–China Reform Forum Conference, Santa Monica, CA, June 28. http://www .rand.org/content/dam/rand/pubs/corporate_pubs/2005/RAND_ CP505.pdf.

Carnell, Brian. 2000. "China to Intensify One Child Effort; Immigration Case Throws Some Horror Stories in Doubt." *Brian.Carnell.com,* September 26. https://brian.carnell.com/articles/2000/china-to -intensify-one-child-effort-immigration-case-throws-some-horror -stories-in-doubt.

Cooper, Richard N. 2005. "Global Public Goods: A Role for China and India." Paper prepared for United Nations Industrial Development Organization International Public Goods for Economic Development project.

Das Gupta, Monica, Jiang Zhenghua, Li Bohua, Xie Zhenming, Woojin Ching, and Bae Hwa-Ok. 2003. "Why Is Son Preference so Persistent in East and South Asia? A Cross-Country Study of China, India, and the Republic of Korea." *Journal of Development Studies* 40 (2): 153–87.

Desai, Prashant, Richard Fairgrieve, Dippanker S. Haldar, A. P. Parigi, and R. Subramanian. 2007. "Tapping into the Indian Consumer Market." Paper presented at the India-Europe Investment Forum, London, June 28.

Golley, Jane, and Rod Tyers. 2006. "China's Growth to 2030: Demographic Change and the Labour Supply Constraint." Working Papers in Economics and Econometrics 467, Australian National University, Canberra.

Hawksworth, John, and Gordon Cookson. 2008. "The World in 2050: Beyond the BRICs; A Broader Look at Emerging Market Growth Prospects." Report for PricewaterhouseCoopers. http://www.pwc.fi /fi_FI/fi/julkaisut/tiedostot/world_in_2050.pdf.

Hofman, Bert, and Louis Kuijs. 2008. "Rebalancing China's Growth." In *Debating China's Exchange Rate Policy*, edited by Morris Goldstein and Nicholas R. Lardy, 109–125. Washington, DC: Peterson Institute for International Economics.

Holz, Carsten A. 2005. "China's Economic Growth, 1978–2025: What We Know Today about China's Economic Growth Tomorrow." EconPapers Development and Comp Systems 0512002. http://128.118.178.162/eps/dev/papers/0512/0512002.pdf.

Huang, Jikun, Linxiu Zhang, Qiang Li, and Huanguang Qiu. 2003. "National and Regional Economic Development Scenarios for China's Food Economy Projections in the Early 21st Century." Report for Center for Chinese Agricultural Policy, Chinese Academy of Sciences.

Laurent, Clint. 2006. *India—Is It the Next China?* Hong Kong: Asian Demographics.

Linn, Johannes F. 2006. "Regional Cooperation and Integration in Central Asia." Report for the Centennial Group.

O'Neill, Jim, Dominic Wilson, Roopa Purushothaman, and Anna Stupnytska. 2005. "How Solid Are the BRICs?" Goldman Sachs Global Economics Paper No. 134. http://www.goldmansachs.com/our-thinking/archive/archive-pdfs/how-solid.pdf.

Paltsev, Sergey, and John Reilly. 2007a. "China and India in Energy Markets and Its Implication for Global Greenhouse Gas Emissions." Paper presented at "India and China's Role in International Trade and Finance and Global Economic Governance" conference, Delhi, India, December 6–7.

———. 2007b. "Energy Scenarios of East Asia: 2005–25." MIT Joint Program on the Science and Policy of Global Change Report No. 152. http://globalchange.mit.edu/files/document/MITJPSPGC_Rpt152.pdf.

Poddar, Tushar, and Eva Yi. 2007. "India's Rising Growth Potential." Goldman Sachs Global Economics Paper No. 152. http://sitemaker.umich.edu/varghese.jacob/files/indias_rising_growth_potential_-_economics_paper_godman_sachs.pdf.

Poncet, Sandra. 2006. "The Long Term Growth Prospects of the World
    Economy: Horizon 2050." CEPII Working Paper No. 2006-16. http://
    www.cepii.fr/%5C/anglaisgraph/workpap/pdf/2006/wp06-16.pdf.
Purushothaman, Roopa. 2004. "India: Realizing BRICs Potential."
    Goldman Sachs Global Economics Paper No. 109.
Quan, Heng. 2008. "Income Inequality in China and India: Structural
    Comparisons." *Asian Scholar*, no. 4. http://www.asianscholarship
    .org/asf/ejourn/articles/Quan%20Heng2.pdf.
Rodrik, Dani, and Arvind Subramanian. 2004. "Why India Can Grow at
    7 Percent a Year or More: Projections and Reflections." International
    Monetary Fund Working Paper WP/04/118.
Shiyang, Cui. 2007. *China: Opportunities, Challenges and Market Entry
    Strategies*. Chengdu, China: US Commercial Service and US
    Consulate General.
Tyers, Rod, Jane Golley, and Iain Bain. 2006. "Projected Economic
    Growth in China and India: The Role of Demographic Change."
    Paper presented at "Shaping the Future: Prospects for Asia's Long
    Term Development over the Next Two Decades" conference,
    Bangkok, December 11–12.
US Department of Energy, Energy Information Administration. 2008.
    International Energy Outlook 2008. Washington, DC: EIA. http://
    www.tulane.edu/~bfleury/envirobio/readings/International
    %20Energy%20Outlook%2008.pdf.
Wilson, Dominic, and Roopa Purushothaman. 2003. "Dreaming with
    BRICs: The Path to 2050." Goldman Sachs Global Economics Paper
    No. 99. http://www.goldmansachs.com/korea/ideas/brics/99
    -dreaming.pdf.
Wilson, Dominic, and Anna Stupnytska. 2007. "The N-11: More than an
    Acronym." Goldman Sachs Global Economics Paper No. 153.
Winters, Alan, and Shahid Yusuf, eds. 2007. *Dancing with Giants: China,
    India, and the Global Economy*. Washington, DC: World Bank Institute
    of Policy Studies.
Wolf, Charles, Jr., and Alisher Akhmedjonov. 2011. "A Macroeconomic
    Assessment." In *China and India, 2025: A Comparative Assessment*,

by Charles Wolf Jr., Siddhartha Dalal, Julie DaVanzo, Eric Larson, Alisher Akhmedjonov, Harun Dogo, Meilinda Huang, and Silvia Montoya, 37–54. Santa Monica, CA: RAND.

Wolf, Charles, Jr., Siddhartha Dalal, Julie DaVanzo, Eric Larson, Alisher Akhmedjonov, Harun Dogo, Meilinda Huang, and Silvia Montoya. 2011. "Population Trends in China and India: Demographic Dividend or Demographic Drag?" In *China and India, 2025: A Comparative Assessment,* 7–35. Santa Monica, CA: RAND.

World Bank. 2007. "Doing Business 2008." http://www.doingbusiness .org/~/media/GIAWB/Doing%20Business/Documents/Annual -Reports/English/DB08-FullReport.pdf.

World Economic Forum. 2006. *China and the World: Scenarios to 2025.* Geneva: World Economic Forum. http://www3.weforum.org/docs /WEF_Scenario_ChinaWorld2025_Report_2010.pdf.

POSTAUDIT

This summary of a RAND study of China and India assessed their respective economic prospects during the next decade. The assessment, originally done in 2009–2011, is both credible and creditable three years later. *Score: Good*

30 Modernizing the North Korean System

Objectives, Method, and Application: Summary

CHARLES WOLF JR. AND NORMAN D. LEVIN

The research project we describe was a collaborative effort among six institutions in five countries: the RAND Corporation in the United States, the POSCO Research Institute (POSRI) and the Research Institute for National Security Affairs (RINSA) in South Korea, the Center for Contemporary Korean Studies (CCKS) at the Institute of World Economy and International Relations (IMEMO) in Russia, the China Reform Forum (CRF) in China, and the Institute for International Policy Studies (IIPS) in Japan. There were three main outcomes. First, the project produced a set of policy instruments that can contribute to modernizing the North Korean system and provide a basis for focused, collaborative efforts to stimulate peaceful change in North Korea. Second, these instruments were integrated into alternative operational plans ("portfolios") and then evaluated in terms of likely responses to the plans' components by the five countries holding talks with North Korea (the six-party talks), spawning a single "consensus plan" that the research partners deemed likely to garner buy-in from their five countries. Third, several potential

This article was previously published as Charles Wolf Jr. and Norman D. Levin, "Summary," in *Modernizing the North Korean System: Objectives, Method, and Application* (Santa Monica, CA: RAND, 2008), xi–xix.

intermediaries—that is, those that could help convey the project findings to one or more levels of the North Korean structure—were identified.

Among the major substantive conclusions with which the research partners agreed were the following:

- The critical challenges posed by North Korea are embedded in the nature of the North Korean system, which diverges significantly from the common benchmarks for modernized, progressing countries.
- Fostering a more normal, or "modernized," country is in the interests of all five of the research partners' countries.
- Modernization entails inherent risks for North Korea that make it, at a minimum, a long-term task. But failure to modernize also entails inherent dangers, and the benefits of modernization will accrue first and foremost to North Korea itself.
- The key requirement for modernization to take place is that of fostering the *aspiration for change* within the North Korean leadership.
- The prerequisite for providing major assistance to North Korea must be successful resolution of the nuclear issue, which means North Korea's complete, verifiable denuclearization.
- In seeking a modernized North Korea, the focus should not be on replacing the North Korean regime but on stimulating the system's gradual modernization.
- The concerned countries should proceed in a comprehensive, step-by-step manner ("action for action"), as is being done in the six-party talks, with time-phased objectives and instruments based on North Korean responses.
- Incentives and disincentives should be strategically targeted at modernizing the system and fostering the aspiration for change within North Korea's leadership.

- Whatever the outcome of the current round of six-party talks, it is imperative that thinking about how to modernize North Korea be done now and that channels be sought for injecting new ways of thinking into the research partner countries' approaches to North Korea and into North Korea itself.

The research method used in this project comprises the four steps summarized in Figure 30.1. The purpose of step I was to produce an inventory of characteristics, or attributes, of the Democratic People's Republic of Korea (DPRK) system that can be broadly identified as archaic, or nonmodern. A nonmodern attribute is one that (1) adversely affects the well-being of the North Korean population, the growth of the North Korean economy, and, indeed, the survival, renewal, and prosperity of the North Korean state, and (2) has been changed for the benefit and more rapid growth of countries that are successfully developing and modernizing, such as South Korea, China, Indonesia, Malaysia, Singapore, and Vietnam.

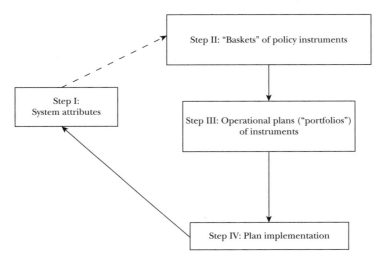

Figure 30.1   Analysis of the North Korean system as a basis for its modernization

Nonmodern attributes pervade the North Korean system's economy, politics, and military establishment. North Korea's nonmodern *economic* attributes include its insular, autarkic trade and investment circumstances; its lack of access to potentially beneficial business transactions; and its lack of access to productive new technologies in agriculture, industry, and services. North Korea's nonmodern *political* attributes include its emphasis on separation from the rest of the world, its institutionalization of one-man rule, and its virtual exclusion from regularized and expanded interactions with other states. Some of the consequences of these political characteristics are severe restrictions on North Korea's access to information technology, to the experience of other countries and governments, and to the advances others have realized in health care and other public services. North Korea's nonmodern *military* attributes all stem from the military establishment's absolute preeminence in the system, which distorts both the economic structure and the rational allocation of resources within it. The by-products of this singular military role include remoteness from military-to-military contacts with other military establishments and a marked inability to benefit from information about the experiences of other countries' military establishments with respect to organization, training, communications, and other ingredients of modern military institutions.

North Korea's existing autarky and insulation have immured it from the rest of the world, whereas the more modern, emerging-market systems have benefited from their integration and interdependence. By its very nature, the North Korean system suppresses sentiment for internal reform and limits diplomatic options for dealing with North Korea's disastrous economic situation.

Step II of our research method entailed identifying a set of potentially modernizing policy instruments and grouping them into separate "baskets" whose components could be variously packaged into alternative operational plans, or "portfolios," for modernizing the North Korean system. Each policy instrument went into a particular basket on the basis of two criteria: (1) it addressed (linked back to) one or more key attributes of the North Korean system that are impeding modernization, and (2) it helped achieve (linked forward to) the overall goal of system modernization by advancing the broad operational objectives for that basket. The four baskets were the following:

- Political basket: introduce new political ideas and promote the system's progressive evolution.
- Economic basket: foster economic opening, transparency, and productive skills.
- Security basket: reduce military threats, enhance military confidence and trust, modulate the role of the military in North Korea, and contribute to regional stability.
- Sociocultural basket: stimulate the advancement of North Korean society and culture by supporting the development of a civil society and encouraging increased priority for social and human needs.

The political basket includes such items as encouraging North Korean participation in international conferences and direct multilateral and bilateral talks between the United States and the DPRK and between Japan and the DPRK, leading to normalization of relations between them. The economic basket includes such measures as liberalizing trade and investment, encouraging economic "experiments" with pilot projects, and establishing property rights and a code for investment and joint business ventures. The security basket includes firm and verifiable denuclearization; prohibition of sales or transfers of nuclear, biological, or chemical (NBC) weapons and technologies; and reciprocal adjustments in the size and deployment of military forces in North and South Korea. Finally, the sociocultural basket includes such items as mutual exchanges by nongovernmental organizations (NGOs) and professional organizations and cultural exchanges and other interactions between religious groups in North Korea and the rest of the world.

Step III of our research method consisted of combining instruments from each basket to form different operational plans, or portfolios, that share the broad objective of contributing to the North Korean system's modernization but seek to accomplish this objective in different ways. Three illustrative plans, each drawing instruments from all baskets, resulted: one emphasizes instruments from the political basket, one emphasizes instruments from the economic basket, and one emphasizes instruments from the security basket. We think of these illustrative plans as portfolios because, in a sense, they are analogous to mutual funds in the financial world. The alternative plans accord different emphases to the four categories of policy instruments in the same way that some mutual funds are designed to accord different emphases to growth versus value stocks, domestic versus international stocks, high-technology versus lower-technology stocks, and so on. The inclusion of important economic instruments in all of the portfolios reflects the fact that any effective plan for modernizing the North Korean system as a whole must address the manifest problems inherent in North Korea's economic system.

Step IV of our method dealt with implementation of the several plans. The concern in this case was the period over which each plan would be implemented; the successive phases, or stages, in which the plan's instruments would be introduced; and the conditionalities, or quid pro quos, that would affect North Korea with relation to measures taken by the other five countries.

All six institutions that collaborated in this research project are relatively independent, scholarly organizations. Given the very diverse national identities of these participants, we found it striking that they shared many assumptions and perspectives related to the broad issues of modernization in North Korea and not surprising that they differed, sometimes sharply, on others. For example, the collaborating institutions shared a conviction that peaceful evolution of the DPRK along "modern" and "normal" lines would be collectively valuable, that a North Korean state possessing nuclear weapons and delivery capabilities would be a serious threat to regional stability, and that possible leakages of NBC weapons from North Korea to terrorist groups would be a serious threat with major consequences for regional and global instability. Yet at the same time, the six institutions displayed several important diverging views—for example, on assessments of whether and in what numbers North Korea already possesses plutonium or highly enriched uranium bombs and delivery systems, on whether multilateral talks and negotiations are likely to be more effective than one-on-one talks or negotiations between North Korea and the United States, and on whether dialogue with North Korea is preferable to dialogue plus pressure (dialogue accompanied by actual or prospective sanctions). Differences of perspective were also evident, both between and within the research teams, on such issues as the extent and significance of North Korea's economic "reforms" and the intentions behind particular North Korean actions.

These differing assumptions and perspectives led to different views on the desirability and feasibility of several of the policy instruments and the operational plans embodying those instruments. This did not, however, prevent the participants from reaching a consensus plan based on shared views and the most widely accepted and agreed-on policy instruments. This plan reflects a shared inclination toward a combined political-security approach focused on gradual system change through reduced threats and increased confidence and mutual trust. It also reflects a shared preference, on the economic side, away from large-scale undertakings and extensive assistance and toward the use of instruments that build self-perpetuating change and implant a different way of thinking among North Koreans. The consensus plan embodies only those instruments that most of the research participants agreed would be both effective in encouraging movement toward modernization in North Korea and likely to gain the support of the participants' governments. No attempt was made to rank instruments according to North Korea's likely receptivity to them, partly because the potential value of particular policy instruments in stimulating modernization does not necessarily hinge on North Korean receptivity and partly because an explicit goal of the research project was to allow North Koreans to undertake such a ranking for themselves.

Table 30.1 summarizes the components of the consensus plan—that is, it shows the embodied instruments from each of the four baskets. The starting point for this plan is the first component of the security basket: verifiable denuclearization of the Korean Peninsula. The participants agreed that in the absence of this component, consideration would have to be given to further tightening or expanding of sanctions and perhaps to adopting additional disincentives (such as new restrictions on North Korean exports or suspension of economic assistance). The consensus plan also includes agreement on steps toward its implementation: Two sequential phases are proposed, each encompassing a mixture of incentives and disincentives, rewards and penalties, and actions taken by North Korea in parallel with actions taken by the five other countries.

In addition to the illustrative operational plans and a consensus plan, the research project provides a method and a tool kit that can be used by entities, groups, or individuals within the North Korean structure to formulate modernization plans of their own that encompass the various instruments and combine them as chosen.

None of the collaborating partners has any illusions about either the ease or the speed with which the chain of events envisaged in

Table 30.1 Consensus plan, derived from shared views
on salient policy instruments

Political basket	Economic basket	Security basket	Sociocultural basket
• Six-nation declaration of nonaggression/peaceful coexistence • Direct multilateral and bilateral (US-DPRK and Japan-DPRK) talks, leading to normalization of relations • DPRK participation in international conferences and institutions	• Encouragement of economic "experiments" and pilot projects • Support for emergence of commercially competitive businesses and commodity markets • Establishment and implementation of code for foreign investment/property rights • Creation of modern financial and budgetary systems, including microfinance • Revenues derived by government to exceed revenues previously derived from illegal/destabilizing activities • Academic/business/NGO exchange programs	• Verifiable denuclearization of Korean Peninsula backed by tightened sanctions, restrictions on North Korean exports, and suspension of economic assistance • US/international security guarantees • Bilateral/multilateral military-to-military security seminars/exercises • Mechanism for ending Korean War and negotiating peace with the regime • Reciprocal adjustments in size/deployment of military forces and other Cooperative Threat Reduction initiatives • Prohibitions of NBC weapons and technology sales/transfers	• Joint programs on medical monitoring, telecommunications, and environment • Academic and cultural/arts exchanges

this research project might ensue. Nevertheless, this provision of a method and an illustration of how such a line of development might occur and a means by which those in North Korea can formulate and pursue such lines on their own can serve to stimulate a modernizing process in North Korea. With this in mind, we plan to produce a Korean-language translation of this report and have it injected through various intermediaries into the North Korean system.

POSTAUDIT

Despite North Korea's continuing provocative activities in "antimodernizing" directions, this summary of a 2008 RAND study of steps that would move North Korea toward modernization remains relevant. The continued relevance derives from the collaborators who participated in the earlier study (including analysts from China, Russia, South Korea, Japan, and RAND) and the study's content. *Score: Good*

---

31 The Cost of Reuniting Korea

Prospects for reuniting South and North Korea may be better than at any time since the demise in 1994 of North Korea's "Great Leader," Kim Il Sung. Several indicators suggest a possible move in this direction.

One indicator is the confiscatory revaluation of the Democratic People's Republic of Korea's currency in 2009. Although the new won's value was pegged at one hundred times the old won, the amounts of wons that could be exchanged and the time period (forty-eight hours) for the exchange were sharply restricted. It's doubtless that some of the ruling elite in the military and government apparatus were severely affected by these confiscatory measures. Their loyalty to Dear Leader Kim Jong Il's rule may be diminishing as a result.

Even though the amount of the new won was sharply reduced, signs of inflation have surfaced. Since revaluation, the market price of rice apparently has doubled over the controlled price, perhaps another sign of loosened control in the Democratic People's Republic of Korea.

This article was previously published as Charles Wolf Jr., "The Cost of Reuniting Korea," *Forbes,* March 15, 2010, http://www.forbes.com/2010/03/15/north-south-korea-asia-reunite-opinions-contributors-charles-wolf-jr.html.

If reunification prospects grow, a major obstacle may arise in the future as it has in the past: concern about the ostensibly enormous costs. The price is especially worrisome to the government in Seoul, in Gyeonggi province, located immediately south of the border and where the burden of refugee flows and their costs would be most acute.

As the United States and other members of the six-party group begin to emerge from the Great Recession, it would be ironic if their willingness to endorse reunification and to share the resulting burden were attenuated by concern over the enormity of the expected costs.

Assuredly, these costs will be large. The good news is that they need not be nearly as large as some have estimated. With careful planning, preparation, and implementation, the costs of Korean reunification can be kept within manageable bounds.

Estimating these costs recalls Winston Churchill's characterization of the Soviet Union: "A riddle wrapped in a mystery inside an enigma." So it's not surprising that estimates made by governments, bankers, and scholars have ranged between less than $100 billion and more than $4 trillion. All of the differing estimates assume that reunification would occur in relatively peaceful circumstances. If reunification occurred during or after war between North and South or extreme violence in the North, the estimates would obviously change.

The principal explanation for the widely varying estimates is the economic goal specified for reunification. A secondary explanation is the relevance (or irrelevance) accorded Germany's precedent.

Most of the prior estimates assume that the goal of reunification must be equalization of per capita gross domestic product (GDP) between North and South Korea. Data for North Korea range between unreliable and apocryphal. However, a reasonable estimate of per capita GDP in the North is perhaps $700, in South Korea about $20,000. The North's population is twenty-four million and South Korea's forty-eight million according to the latest census. Linking these disparities to a goal of raising per capita GDP in the North to that in the South and assuming a medium capital requirement of $4 per unit increase in North Korea's GDP results in estimated reunification costs of $1.9 trillion.[1]

If a more modest goal is adopted focusing on dramatically increasing per capita income in the North—say, by doubling it within five or six years—instead of equalization with the South, the cost burden decreases sharply to $62 billion. The goal and the resulting reunification costs are more modest and more feasible. Arguably, the reassuring experience of a tangible doubling of living standards in the North combined with the forbidding uncertainties that would attach to possible emigration are also likely to minimize southward refugee flows.

The costs of Germany's reunification are both frequently cited and largely irrelevant. This is because the economic policies adopted by the West German government after the Berlin Wall fell in 1989 simply decreed for immediate political reasons that wages, pensions, and other entitlements for East German citizens must equal those in West Germany. Germany committed itself to paying the bills. They continue to arrive, currently totaling $3 trillion and still counting.

To be sure, adopting the more modest but still ambitious goal of rapidly doubling per capita GDP would leave a reunified Korea with sharp disparities between North and South. How far and how quickly Korea would move toward reducing these disparities would no doubt be a top priority of the Korean state. Still, there are many instances of countries and governments that have faced large economic, political, and social disparities while functioning with tolerable stability and effectiveness. These instances include Belgium (the Flemish and Walloons), Italy (prosperous Piemonte and poorer Mezzogiorno), Indonesia (in Ambon), and the United States (California and Mississippi).

If and when Korean reunification occurs, the costs will most heavily impact South Korea. But the burden can and should be shared with Korea's American ally and with the other principals engaged in the six-party talks, including China and Japan. If reunification ensues on the heels of the current Great Recession, the burdens are more likely to be amicably borne if the costs are realistically bounded.

Note

1. For further details, see Charles Wolf Jr. and Kamil Akramov, "North Korean Paradoxes: Circumstances, Costs, and Consequences of Korean Reunification," RAND MG-333, 2005.

POSTAUDIT

This 2010 *Forbes* article suggests that the costs of potential Korean unification have been grossly overestimated—by inappropriately drawing on the experience of German reunification. The essay also suggests specific measures that would enable these costs to be substantially reduced and shared among several countries in addition to South Korea. *Score: Good*

PART V

Other Regions and Issues

32 Austerity and Stimulus— Two Misfires

Why is it that in the United States the "stimulus" solution to the economy's ills has performed badly while in Europe the opposite approach, "austerity," has performed even worse?

The answer is that austerity (defined as substantial reductions in debt-financed government spending) or stimulus (defined as high levels of debt-financed government spending) will promote growth only in some countries and in some circumstances.

Whether either policy will work depends critically on the responses of the private sector. What is missing from consideration today is whether the private sector's reactions will enhance, retard, or reverse either a policy of austerity or of stimulus. In both the European Union and the United States, policies would have been more effective if efforts had been made to anticipate and mitigate the reasons for adverse responses of private businesses.

Four years since the Great Recession ended in mid-2009, and notwithstanding recent signs of modest improvements, the annual rate of real US gross domestic product (GDP) growth has averaged less than 2 percent—which is four percentage points, or $600 billion, below the pace of recovery from prior deep recessions, such

This article was previously published as Charles Wolf Jr., "Austerity and Stimulus— Two Misfires," *Wall Street Journal*, May 21, 2013, http://on.wsj.com/15Ik3qv.

as in 1981–1982. Recorded unemployment is 7.5 percent but is actually twice as high when allowing for involuntary temporary and part-time employment and discouraged workers who have stopped looking for work.

The stimulus of 2009–2012 averaged over 6 percent of GDP annually—between $1.2 trillion and $1.5 trillion. Yet it has been ineffective.

Austerity in the European Union has fared even worse. In the euro-currency area, which includes eighteen of the European Union's twenty-seven members, government spending has been cut in half, with dire consequences. GDP growth is at a standstill, and recorded unemployment is 12 percent and rising.

Yet true believers in either policy, which include Nobel Prize winners on both sides, discount the results. Stimulus adherents claim that the poor record simply reflects that the recession was so deep that the stimulus should have been even bigger. Austerity adherents claim that its dismal record simply reflects that it was too severe and imposed too quickly.

Both groups are overlooking the crucial role of the private sector's reactions to austerity and stimulus.

In the United States, these reactions are crucial because the private sector's size is so large—the majority shareholder, so to speak. Its share of purchased goods and services is approximately quadruple that of government. Several factors are at work. One is what textbooks refer to as "Ricardian equivalence"—that debt-financed government spending in the present may require higher taxes in the future, thereby motivating companies and households to save rather than invest or spend.

An indicator of this is the ballooning of cash reserves on corporate balance sheets to over $2 trillion since 2009, thereby providing a major offset to the stimulus goal of expanding aggregate demand. Other indicators are increased household savings rates (by 3–4 percent annually) since 2009 and decreased household debt (by 8 percent), thus further negating the increased aggregate demand sought by stimulus.

Another impediment is the quandary created for business plans because of uncertainty about where and how stimulus would affect each firm's markets and those of its competitors—uncertainty that is magnified when stimulus is accompanied by profuse, costly, and ambiguous regulations.

Finally, stimulus in the United States has been undercut by private-investment decisions to invest abroad. Between the recession's turnaround in mid-2009 and the end of 2012, outward-bound US private direct investment rose steadily to $1.73 trillion annually from $1.05 trillion. This outward-bound investment currently exceeds (by $500 billion) the outward flow preceding the recession in 2007.

Private-sector reactions in Europe have also seriously affected austerity's results. The European Union's private sector is smaller relative to government than it is in the United States—about three to two versus four to one. Moreover, the direct involvement of government is more pervasive than in the United States. For example, European governments are often part owners of private corporations and sometimes sit on corporate boards.

Austerity in the European Union has imposed simultaneous and severe spending cuts on the government and the private economy, thereby reducing opportunities for either one to cushion the adverse impact of austerity on the other. The European Union's private businesses also seem less enabling of entrepreneurship and innovation that could facilitate adjustment to austerity.

Neither in the United States nor in the European Union does the "private sector" speak with one voice or necessarily react in a uniform way. For example, some venture-capital firms and other wealth-management companies in the United States have reacted less adversely to government policy than others. Still, the experience to date strongly suggests that the reactions and behavior of private investors and consumers to stimulus in the United States and to austerity in the European Union critically affected each policy's tarnished record. Something for policy makers to keep in mind when devising economic remedies.

POSTAUDIT

Failure to anticipate and to ameliorate the private sector's response accounts in large measure for the ineffectiveness of austerity policies in Europe and of stimulus policies in the United States. I think this op-ed, written in 2013, remains convincing. *Score: Good*

33 How Might bin Laden's Demise Affect Business?

Given how markets are responding thus far, Osama bin Laden's death is likely to have a modestly positive and buoyant effect on equity markets. Business abhors uncertainty. With bin Laden gone, one major source of uncertainty is removed, along, one hopes, with his hallmark of large-scale coordinated violence.

A net positive effect may ensue in Libya. On one hand, Muammar Qaddafi claims al Qaeda as an adversary, so bin Laden's elimination might be construed as adding to the Libyan tyrant's self-confidence and sense of his own endurance. On the other hand, the deadly and deft force wielded by the United States in taking down one bitter enemy could undermine Qaddafi's confidence in his own survival and encourage his willingness to depart. If bin Laden's takedown hastens Qaddafi's departure, Libya's relatively small contribution to global oil supplies is likely to resume. In that case, uncertainties may also abate among the larger oil suppliers, and rising oil futures prices may be reversed. We are already seeing signs of this sequence.

Any positive effects of bin Laden's death could be offset by plausible worries over terrorist acts galvanized by elements of the

This article was previously published as Charles Wolf Jr., "How Might bin Laden's Demise Affect Business?" *RAND Blog*, May 25, 2011, http://www.rand.org /blog/2011/05/how-might-bin-ladens-demise-affect-business.html.

al Qaeda network in Yemen, the Arabian Peninsula, Pakistan, and Indonesia. These terrorist enclaves may vie for stature or seek to exalt bin Laden's status as a martyr by stepping up their own terrorist acts. A flurry of smaller-scale, but numerous and widely dispersed, terrorist acts could have a chilling effect on global direct investment.

Another chain of events more conjectural than those described, yet possibly more potent than all of them together, concerns how bin Laden's demise will affect the financing of international terrorism. Some putative terrorism experts had viewed bin Laden dismissively as a voice from the past and one whose influence had waned as al Qaeda evolved toward its more decentralized current structure. Their conclusion was that bin Laden's demise would not have much, if any, effect on the risks of terrorist acts because these are undertaken by the separate entities in the network.

That was before the United States captured his hard drives and other records that revealed bin Laden's direct involvement in planning terrorist activity from within his walled compound. The circumstances surrounding his location and his modus operandi reminded us that he has been the principal fundraiser for global terrorism from Morocco to Indonesia and from Europe to the United States. It is not coincidental that two brothers (now deceased) who owned the bin Laden compound in Abbottabad were professional moneychangers (*hawala* system). Neither is it implausible that one of the brothers had been bin Laden's trusted courier for many years, presumably functioning in the *hawala* circuit as both recipient and dispenser of the largesse that bin Laden's unique status attracted, in addition to subventions financed by his personal wealth.

Dramatic, large-scale terrorist acts depend on the availability of adequate financing to cover their costs of planning, recruiting, training, and equipment. Because bin Laden's demise is likely to disrupt the sources of funding, it may be reasonable to expect a diminution in the numbers and scale of such acts. If his followers respond with smaller-scale terrorist acts, these may be more readily managed by seasoned law enforcement. The risks of small-scale attacks are sometimes insurable, and indeed precedents in insuring against such risks already exist in the experience and practices of Lloyds, Allianz, and AIG. It is to be hoped, if not confidently forecasted, that business will be encouraged as a result.

POSTAUDIT

This conjectural piece on repercussions ensuing from Osama bin Laden's demise shows limited prescience and limited relevance. It has been largely overtaken by events. *Score: Not good*

34 Enhancement by Enlargement

The Proliferation Security Initiative: Summary

CHARLES WOLF JR., BRIAN G. CHOW,
AND GREGORY S. JONES

The Proliferation Security Initiative (PSI), begun in 2003, was conceived as an activity rather than an organization, the intention being to focus on collective action while avoiding the bureaucratic impediments that organizations often entail. PSI's purpose is to prevent or at least inhibit the spread of weapons of mass destruction (WMD), their delivery systems, and related materials to or from states or nonstate actors whose possession of such items would be a serious threat to global or regional security. An Operational Experts Group (OEG) of twenty countries leads the initiative's operations, planning and implementing the exercises and other multilateral efforts designed to further PSI's purpose. Ninety-one countries, including the OEG members, make up this group of widely multilateral participants, all of which have endorsed PSI's purpose and principles.

This RAND project for the US secretary of defense's Policy Office had two objectives. The first was to assess the advantages and disadvantages, or benefits and costs, that when balanced against each other have induced five key countries not to affiliate

This article was previously published as Charles Wolf Jr., Brian G. Chow, and Gregory S. Jones, "Summary," in *Enhancement by Enlargement: The Proliferation Security Initiative* (Santa Monica, CA: RAND, 2008), vii–xiv.

with PSI publicly, and the second was to ascertain whether (and, if so, how) this balance might be altered to enhance the prospects for their affiliation in the near future. Implicit in this objective is the premise that PSI's effectiveness will be enhanced by enlarging the number of participants.

The project's second objective was to develop a syllabus of training materials, partly by drawing on work done in connection with the first objective. The syllabus is intended to help US Geographic Combat Commands mitigate problems arising from normal staff turnover and insufficient institutional memory and thereby to improve the commands' ability to provide operational support for the numerous multilateral exercises constituting the core of PSI's peacetime activities.

We address the first objective in this report; the second will be addressed in a separate document that also provides additional details about PSI and about relevant treaties, agreements, and programs discussed in this report.

The five countries of interest—Indonesia, Malaysia, Pakistan, India, and China—share an implicit calculus that the costs (disadvantages) associated with PSI affiliation exceed, or at least equal, the benefits (advantages). We identify specific issues within these countries' assessments for which the benefits ascribed to PSI might have been underestimated or the costs ascribed to PSI overestimated or both. We then suggest how these under- and overestimates might be changed in ways that would lead these countries to reconsider their decision not to affiliate with PSI. Of course, if these countries see their estimates as correct and not subject to reconsideration, it follows that their nonaffiliated PSI status will remain unchanged.

The Five Countries

We begin by dividing the five countries into three groups: Indonesia and Malaysia; Pakistan and India; and China. These groupings reflect the conjecture that the probability of one member in a two-member group (the group of one does not play in this conjecture) changing its stance of nonaffiliation with PSI is likely to be affected by whether the other member of that group alters its stance. However, these groupings preclude neither the possibility of interactions between countries in the different groups nor the possibility of significant interactions with countries other than these five. Indeed, interactions between Saudi Arabia, which endorsed PSI in May 2008, and India and Pakistan remain relevant to India's and Pakistan's assessments of whether to endorse PSI.

In analyzing the five countries' decisions, we have attempted to adopt their separate perspectives and sensitivities to better understand why or how each might have overestimated the disadvantages or underestimated the advantages of PSI affiliation. For example, to the extent that China views PSI as a US-dominated activity and continues seeking to strengthen the Shanghai Cooperation Organisation as a counterweight to the United States in Asia, China may conclude that nonaffiliation is the preferable stance.

In considering the first group, Indonesia and Malaysia, we begin by describing their interdependencies and shared interests. We then turn to three salient issues and concerns they both have that have so far led them to refrain from formal PSI affiliation: sovereignty, law of the sea, and independent foreign policy.

The two members of the second group, Pakistan and India, are current nuclear powers that, in certain circumstances, might have reasons and resources that would dispose them to assist Saudi Arabia if it sought to acquire a nuclear capability of its own (perhaps in response to such an acquisition by Iran). One of the several intricate interactions among the three is that the nexus between the possible interest in future acquisition by the Saudis and the possible sources of future supply represented by Pakistan or India might influence Pakistan and India to avoid or at least defer PSI affiliation. However, in the case of India, internal political circumstances are currently much more formidable obstacles to joining PSI.

We chose to treat China separately for several reasons. In addition to being a nuclear weapon state, it is the second- or third-largest economy in the world, the fourth- or fifth-largest global trading country, and the third- or fourth-largest global weapons exporter. Moreover, it has a mixture of political, economic, and security interests and transactions with North Korea and Iran, the two major current and prospective sources of "proliferation concern" in the world. The mixture and complexity of interests at stake for China include a prevalent belief among its leadership that blandness and "carrots" rather than coercion and "sticks" enhance its ability to influence North Korea and that affiliation with PSI would, by appearing threatening to North Korea, compromise this ability.

China's inclination toward Iran is similar—it seeks to temporize rather than pressure. China's estimate of the consequences of PSI affiliation may also be influenced by reluctance to jeopardize its substantial and growing trade and investment transactions with Iran.

The Five Principles

After a broad assessment of the general and specific benefits that countries typically associate with PSI affiliation, we address the key policy question of this research: What measures, policies, and approaches can the United States and other PSI participants invoke that are likely to induce each of the five countries to lower its estimates of PSI-affiliation costs (disadvantages) or raise its estimates of PSI-affiliation benefits (advantages) such that it arrives at a positive (rather than negative or neutral) bottom-line estimate?

To assist us in answering this question, we set out five general principles to use as guides in seeking remedial policies conducive to PSI affiliation by the five countries. Each principle applies to at least one of the five countries; several apply jointly to more than one country. These principles are as follow:

1. Exercising US leadership by ceding it to other PSI participants
2. Interpreting and applying "innocent passage" consistent with each state's own national legal authorizations and its obligations under international law
3. Affirming the validity of territorial waters and emphasizing the locus of responsibility in the littoral countries
4. Presenting PSI affiliation as incremental to agreements or commitments already arrived at
5. Conferring membership in the OEG ab initio.

Note that our five principles do not include carrots and sticks related to issues outside PSI, such as peaceful nuclear assistance for nuclear power plants. Instead, they focus on assuring the five countries that PSI participation will not interfere with their existing international obligations and rights, which should enable them to reassess the costs and benefits of PSI affiliation. Our objective is for the five to affiliate with PSI because they consider the benefits of doing so to outweigh the costs—not because they want to use the act of affiliation as a bargaining chip for obtaining benefits or avoiding penalties on issues unrelated to PSI or nonproliferation. Affiliation for its own sake will make them more active participants and, in the long run, will meet the nonproliferation objective far better than affiliation for extraneous reasons.

Applying the Five Principles

Our next step was to apply the principles to each of the countries, in the process considering how application might alter the calculus of costs and benefits of PSI affiliation. The aim and the result of this exercise were the same: to suggest the manner in which each country should be approached and the points that should be highlighted in inviting each one to join PSI.

Indonesia and Malaysia

It would be prudent for the PSI invitations extended to Indonesia and Malaysia to come from Singapore, Japan, France, Australia, and one or two states in the Gulf Cooperation Council (principle 1). Acting on behalf of the full PSI constituency, these countries would explicate the subjectivity of determining what may or may not be innocent passage (principle 2) and the unambiguous protection of territorial waters by the littoral states (principle 3). New Zealand might usefully be included among the several countries extending the invitation, partly because of its geographic proximity and partly because it has effectively articulated the broad scope of benefits from PSI affiliation.

Given these two countries' viewpoints on the United States, it may be advisable to pursue this approach initially with Malaysia and then with Indonesia. Moreover, approaching Malaysia first would benefit from the fact that Malaysia has already been an observer in three PSI exercises and has joined the Container Security Initiative (CSI). This is an application of principle 4 for building on the five countries' relevant prior activities, including their recent efforts to enact domestic laws and to join international agreements for nonproliferation. Although Indonesia has not observed any PSI exercises or joined CSI, it has made recent efforts along similar lines, both domestically and internationally, in support of nonproliferation. Moreover, because of Indonesia's stature and strategic location, its invitation should include an offer of immediate membership in the OEG.

India and Pakistan

It may be advisable to have France, the United Kingdom, and Russia—the three nuclear-state PSI participants other than the United States—and perhaps Japan, convey invitations to India and Pakistan. Having the United States forgo this role of formal protagonist (principle 1) may help allay India's sensitivity by emphasizing the multilateral character of PSI's activities and modulating the US role in them.

The protagonists should assure India and Pakistan (and the other three countries as well) that PSI will not compromise their right of innocent passage (principle 2). The incremental character of PSI affiliation should be emphasized in light of these countries' prior efforts to enact domestic laws and to join international agreements for nonproliferation (principle 4). For example, Pakistan has already participated as an observer in three PSI exercises, India in two. Finally, it would be appropriate and perhaps more effective if the invitation to both India and Pakistan were accompanied by an option for immediate participation in the PSI's OEG (principle 5).

China

China's affiliation with PSI should be sought by several principal PSI members, including but not confined to the United States. The invitation's effectiveness would be enhanced if, for example, it were extended jointly by France, the United Kingdom, Germany, and the United States, with the first three playing the lead role (principle 1). France and perhaps Russia, as another PSI member, might authoritatively convey the consistency between PSI affiliation, on one hand, and the appropriate and reasonable qualifications within PSI's interdiction principles that can be invoked to protect the right of genuinely innocent passage, on the other (principle 2).

With China, the United States may be in the best position to explicate the incremental and complementary nature of PSI affiliation (principle 4). In the last two decades, China has taken part in many international nonproliferation treaties and agreements. Also, China has already placed three of its principal ports (Hong Kong, Shanghai, and Shenzhen) under the purview of CSI. Consequently, PSI can be accurately portrayed as only a modest additional step that complements China's other nonproliferation efforts. The persuasiveness of China's invitation is likely to be enhanced by having all four of the inviting powers extend the option of immediate status in the OEG upon affiliation (principle 5).

Preliminary Ideas for Further Consideration

We also provide, for further consideration, some preliminary ideas on PSI's development and, more specifically, on the pros and cons of PSI affiliation:

- Discussing with the insurance industry whether and, if so, how premiums charged for insuring cargo (whether transported by surface, air, or sea) take into account any risk abatement related to affiliation with PSI of the transport vehicle's nation of origin
- Considering ways to allay concerns about the right of innocent passage, especially the concern that an innocent ship might suffer delay because of interdiction
- Clarifying possible misinterpretation about the relationship between the United Nations Convention on the Law of the Sea and PSI with respect to the right of innocent passage, including appropriate rules of engagement that would

reassure littoral states that their prerogatives in their own territorial seas would not be infringed by PSI interdiction principles

- Considering whether to offer prospective PSI members technical assistance, inspection equipment, and other items that might help improve their import-export control, inspection, and interdiction capabilities
- Analyzing the status and trends of technology for sensing and detecting WMD that may enable better and quicker identification of WMD components, thereby enhancing the effectiveness of PSI

POSTAUDIT

PSI is remarkably (and fortunately) underreported in the press, notwithstanding that nearly one hundred countries participate. This summary of a RAND study of PSI and possible ways to encourage several prominent hold-out countries to affiliate remains timely. *Score: Good*

35 Asia's Nonproliferation Laggards

China, India, Pakistan, Indonesia, and Malaysia

The proliferation of weapons of mass destruction (WMD) ranks as one of the biggest challenges facing the Obama administration. Luckily, Mr. Obama has a tool to combat this threat, in the form of the Proliferation Security Initiative (PSI), a nontreaty, multilateral initiative that over ninety countries have joined. The trick now will be to convince key Asian countries—China, India, Pakistan, Indonesia, and Malaysia—to participate.

PSI was one of the great successes of the George W. Bush administration. Formed in 2003, it was explicitly conceived as an activity rather than a formal organization to signify its focus on collective action. PSI has none of the bureaucratic baggage of multilateral institutions. Its major activities thus far include more than thirty-five maritime, air, and ground interdiction exercises conducted under its auspices and involving seventy PSI-affiliated countries. The broad aim of these exercises is to enhance national capabilities for sharing and acting on intelligence information; streamlining and coordinating customs procedures; and identifying and

This article was previously published as Charles Wolf Jr., "Asia's Nonproliferation Laggards: China, India, Pakistan, Indonesia and Malaysia," *Wall Street Journal Asia*, February 9, 2009, http://www.rand.org/blog/2009/02/asias-nonproliferation-laggards-china-india-pakistan.html.

interdicting traffic involving WMD, their delivery systems, and their components.

PSI has grown rapidly and counts ninety-one countries among its members today. That figure reflects the appeal of this focus and provides tangible evidence of America's propensity to favor multilateral rather than unilateral action, contrary to conventional wisdom. It has also scored some big wins; for instance, PSI contributed notably to bringing down Pakistan's A. Q. Khan nuclear proliferation network in 2004.

However, the need to expand PSI is still pressing. The demand for WMD remains strong, and the consequences of such weapons getting into the wrong hands are becoming more hazardous daily. If Iran's Shiites obtain nuclear weapons, that may spark arms races with Sunni Saudi Arabia and Egypt. Stateless entities such as Hamas and Hezbollah, perhaps with financial resources from Iran, may also seek weapons. WMD in the wrong hands could make eruptions such as Lebanon in 2006 or Gaza in 2008 catastrophic.

On the supply side, PSI's concern centers on "states of proliferation concern"—a euphemism for North Korea and Iran. North Korea already possesses nuclear technology and weapons, probably between six and eight bombs. Although Pyongyang previously indicated willingness to discontinue its program for plutonium-fueled weapons in return for tangible compensation from its negotiating partners in the six-party talks, that offer no longer appears to be on the table. Iran's capabilities lag those of North Korea with respect to plutonium technology but probably lead with respect to enrichment of uranium as a potential weapon fuel. Both states are in dire economic straits and may proliferate WMD technology to ease their financial predicament.

Pakistan is another country that might be drawn into the supply side of the WMD market by a combination of desperate economic circumstances and internal political instability. While such an adverse development seems remote, the history of the A. Q. Khan network and Pakistan's parlous current political situation are not reassuring.

Given this outcome, the fact that five key Asian countries remain outside the PSI framework is both puzzling and worrisome. A recent RAND study, which I led, attempts to fathom the reasons underlying their concerns—a mixture of possible misunderstanding of the permissive nature of PSI activities and uncertainty about the ensuing political fallout from PSI affiliation—and to suggest possible remedies.

Reasons for not yet endorsing PSI differ among the five Asian countries. Their most salient concerns include worries about breaching the UN Convention on the Law of the Sea, adversely affecting political or financial relations with Iran or North Korea, and implicit subservience to what at its inception appeared to be a US-dominated initiative. For the littoral countries among the five—Indonesia and Malaysia—reluctance to affiliate with PSI is abetted by sensitivities regarding sovereignty over their territorial waters, which they don't want compromised. The Barack Obama administration, through delicate diplomacy, can alleviate these misplaced concerns by clarifying the limited and flexible character of PSI and explaining the collective and collegial character of PSI decision making.

Strengthening PSI, along with diplomacy, the threat of sanctions, and the incentive of economic cooperation, should be high on the priorities of the Obama administration in Washington and in other governments that have large stakes in a less minatory international environment.

POSTAUDIT

The threat of proliferation and hence the relevance of PSI as a counter have increased rather than abated in the five years since this was written. *Score: Good*

36 Natural Disasters

Economically speaking, are natural disasters net contractionary or stimulative events?

In the near term, natural disasters are unambiguously contractionary. Japan's triple earthquake, tsunami, and nuclear disasters since March 2011 have contracted Japan's gross domestic product by 2–3 percent.

But in the medium and longer terms, and under favorable conditions, natural disasters can be stimulative (for example, following China's Chengdu earthquake in 2008, Indonesia's Sumatran tsunami in 2004, and South Korea's separation from the North in the 1950s—the latter both a natural and unnatural disaster).

So perhaps it may be better to pose the question another way: Under what conditions are natural disasters likely to be net stimulative?

In addition to a longer time horizon, the stimulative conditions include (1) possibly enhanced motivations for both government and the private sector to mobilize expanded investment to meet priority needs, (2) opportunities to modernize technology and

This excerpt was previously published in "Natural Disasters: The Views of Seventeen Important Thinkers," *International Economy*, Summer 2011, 38.

increase productivity along with the package of replacement and repair of damages wrought by the disaster, (3) galvanized foreign assistance (both financial and technical and from both governmental and nongovernmental sources), and (4) unity and cohesion of political leadership, public solidarity, and public policy (perhaps supplanting a predisaster regimen of divisiveness and wrangling).

Absent these stimulative conditions, the contractionary effects of natural disasters may well endure, including persistently weakened consumer demand resulting from lingering fears and uncertainties induced by the disaster, more risk-averse investors enfeebled by the disaster's aftereffects, and possible emigration of "best and brightest" from the impacted country or area.

As a wild guess, I'd opine that the stimulative effects are likely to predominate in Japan, the contractionary effects more likely to predominate in Haiti, and the effects in the United States lurk somewhere in between.

POSTAUDIT

Whether natural disasters have increased in frequency or severity or whether they are simply more fully and frequently reported and publicized is unclear. This brief appraisal, written in 2011, of their short-term and longer-term economic effects remains relevant. What's missing is consideration of the perhaps differing effects of clustered disasters. *Score: Medium*

37   The Economist's Pantheon

Charles Wolf Jr. on Grand Pursuit: The Story of Economic Genius *by Sylvia Nasar*

Sylvia Nasar's account of the Great Depression has a disturbing resonance with the Great Recession of 2007 to 2009 and our anemic recovery from it. In *Grand Pursuit,* she recounts an array of public policy interventions by the economists and economic commentariat of the time (including John Maynard Keynes, Irving Fisher, Felix Frankfurter, and occasionally Friedrich Hayek and Joseph Schumpeter). The wide range of their often-conflicting views was not that different from the contemporary commentariat (including Paul Krugman and Larry Summers, on one side, and Gregory Mankiw, Robert Barro, and Michael Boskin, on the other).

Keynes, in an open letter to President Franklin Roosevelt published in the *New York Times* in May 1933, explicitly urged the president to pursue deficit spending of 8 percent of gross domestic product (GDP) as a federal stimulus program (about 50 percent larger as a share of GDP than the Barack Obama stimulus spending of 2009–2010). His recommendation included a confident forecast that this stimulus would "increase national income

This article was previously published as Charles Wolf Jr., "The Economist's Pantheon," *Policy Review,* March 30, 2012, http://www.hoover.org/research/economists-pantheon.

by at least three or four times this amount . . . because [of the]
. . . Multiplier—the cumulative effect of increased individual
incomes[, which] . . . improves the incomes of a further set of
recipients and so on."

Keynes's optimistic forecast brings to mind similar forecasts by
contemporary Keynesians. It also brings to mind the directly contradictory empirical work of Barro and Boskin showing negative
or nugatory stimulus effects from deficit financing of expanded
government spending. It also suggests a theoretical flaw in the
Keynesian model that is not addressed by Nasar. I'll have more to
say about this flaw later in this review.

The resonance between then and now gives fresh meaning to
the familiar aphorism *plus ça change, plus c'est la même chose*—or, in
the same vein, the Yogi Berra version: "It's déjà vu, all over again!"

Sylvia Nasar, a former economics correspondent for the *New
York Times* and current professor at Columbia's Graduate School
of Journalism, also wrote *A Beautiful Mind,* the biography of one-
time mathematician, turned game theorist, turned economist,
and Nobel Prize recipient John Nash. *Grand Pursuit* is more expansive and more ambitious, as well as more cursory, than the sharply
focused Nash biography.

The narrative of *Grand Pursuit* traverses nearly two centuries
of economic thought and economic history. Its successive chapters describe the work of Karl Marx, Friedrich Engels, Alfred
Marshall, Beatrice and Sidney Webb, Fisher, Schumpeter, Keynes,
and Hayek, as well as several lesser luminaries including Ludwig
von Mises, Milton Friedman, Paul Samuelson, Joan Robinson, and
Amartya Sen. Nasar's account focuses especially on the social and
political environment in which these economists developed their
thinking, rather than the more strictly economic content of their
work. Consequently, *Grand Pursuit* may be of particular interest
to political scientists, sociologists, historians, and other social scientists rather than economists. Schumpeter's own little book, *Ten*

Great Economists (1951), and more recently Nicholas Wapshott's *Keynes Hayek: The Clash That Defined Modern Economics* (2011) contain more of the nitty-gritty of economics in their overviews of economic history and economic thought.

Reflecting Nasar's interest in the political and social context of the times, several themes emerge from the book's broad sweep.

One is the change that economics embraced and helped energize from the Dickensian and Malthusian world in which poverty and misery were assumed to be permanent and predominant. Nasar suggests that economists from the mid-nineteenth century sought explanations of why substantial improvements in human well-being had actually occurred and whether and how the trend might be sustained. Marx lodged the explanation in exploitation and imperialism and erroneously predicted violent collapse of the capitalist system. Alfred Marshall, though, suggested that the explanation for the improvements that had occurred was the dramatic increase in labor productivity. He thereby envisioned a major direction for the further development of modern economics.

Another theme that recurs in the book's account of economists' thinking is their accompanying concern about inequality, along with their occasional recognition of the more subtle distinction between inequality and inequity—a distinction often overlooked in much of our current discussion of the subject. The Webbs, Harold Laski, and other Fabian socialists at the London School of Economics saw the prevalence of inequality as a symptom of "class war." To relieve the egregious evidence of inequality in England, they advocated development of what Beatrice Webb called "the Housekeeping State," the precursor of what became the modern welfare state. In Nasar's account of economists' thinking about inequality, Keynes subsequently and unequivocally "rejected the politics of class war." His rejection focused especially on the Labour Party, with which the Webbs were associated. Keynes condemned what he described as that party's opposition "to anyone who is more successful, more skillful, and more industrious, more thrifty than the average." Keynes, somewhat imperiously, criticized it as "a class Party," adding that "the Party is not my Party. I can be influenced . . . by . . . justice and good sense, but the class war will find me on the side of the educated bourgeoisie."

A third theme is the instability of prices and employment, inflation and deflation, the business cycle, the recurrence of "booms and busts"—and what to do about them. Fisher claimed that expanded credit was the main cause of booms and the crunch of debt repayment the main precipitant of busts. Milton Friedman (and his coauthor and wife Anna Schwarz) found instead that the peaks and troughs in America's instability were preceded by contractions of the money supply or its rate of growth (along with considerable uncertainty as to what was cause and what was effect).

To this broad theme of economic instability Schumpeter brought a vision of both causes of the booms and remedies (or at least palliatives) for the busts. The ingredients of Schumpeter's *Theory of Economic Development* are innovation, entrepreneurship, and credit. Schumpeter advanced the classic Marshallian emphasis on increased productivity by emphasizing as the distinctive feature of capitalism "incessant innovation" and "the perennial gale of creative destruction." In Nasar's account, "Schumpeter focused on the human element," finding that "[economic] development depended primarily on entrepreneurship," and "shar[ed] the obsession of late nineteenth-century German culture with leadership." The entrepreneur's essential function was, in Schumpeter's words, "to revolutionize the pattern of production" and to use "an untried technological possibility . . . to destroy old patterns of thought and action." Exceptional abilities and exceptional people were required for these tasks. As set forth in Schumpeter's *Theory*, "carrying out a new plan and acting according to a customary one are things as different as making a road and walking along it."

Nasar writes that in Schumpeter's view "entrepreneurs did more to eliminate poverty than any government or charity." For entrepreneurship to thrive required a propitious environment including, as Schumpeter saw it, property rights, free trade, stable currencies, and especially, cheap and abundant credit provided by "bankers and other financial middlemen who mobilize savings, evaluate projects, manage risk, monitor managers, acquire facilities and otherwise redirected resources from old to new channels." Nasar further describes Schumpeter's thinking: The entrepreneur's dependence on the financial sector and that "sector's peculiar dependence on confidence and trust made it vulnerable to panics and crashes. . . . What distinguished successful economies was not the absence of crises and slumps" but that these economies "more than made up lost ground during investment booms."

Nasar's perceptive conclusion to this exposition of Schumpeter's thinking is worth quotation because of its relevance to the current predicament of the postrecession US economy:

> By emphasizing the local business environment . . . Schumpeter's theory suggested that nations made their own destinies. Governments that wished to see their citizens prosper should . . . focus on fostering a favorable business climate—strong property rights, stable prices, free trade, moderate taxes, and consistent regulation—for entrepreneurs. . . . His was an equal opportunity, optimistic, and, not coincidentally, unwarlike formula for economic success.

One more theme that leaps from the pages of *Grand Pursuit* is the frequency and ease with which the principal members of Nasar's cast of characters crossed the borders between their sequestered academic purlieus and the open, free-for-all fields of politics and the media. Keynes through the *New Statesman* journal, but also through innumerable other news outlets, was an indefatigable source in the public media. So, too, were the Webbs,

Fisher, Friedman, Samuelson, Sen, and, to a lesser extent, Hayek and Schumpeter. Whether their main motivation for these border crossings was to increase the policy impact of their scholarly work, or to spring free of scholarly constraints, or to realize some personal ego gratification, or perhaps a combination of all of these, the reality is they all tended toward public advocacy apart from their scholarly endeavors.

Most of the economists who populate Nasar's book were energetic publicists, pamphleteers, and public letter writers, as well as economic scholars. It's also worth noting that, when some stalwart economists shifted their attention to public commentary, the link between their scholarly work and their policy stances often vanished. For example, Robert Solow's principal scholarly contribution suggested that 90 percent of the increase in US labor productivity in the first half of the twentieth century was due to technological progress, innovation, and (inferentially at least) entrepreneurship. Logically, this important empirical finding should have placed Solow's policy stance squarely in the Schumpeterian camp. Yet in his public commentary, Solow has been an unrelenting Keynesian, echoing calls for expanded deficit financing of government stimulus programs, while (in Nasar's understated words) "dismiss[ing] Schumpeter, rather unfairly." The grasp of their ideological commitment is sometimes no less relenting among scholars than it is among those with weaker intellectual credentials. Whatever the outlandish one-track emanations from Krugman in his biweekly diatribes (which, like the Solow example, actually have no connection with his own scholarly work), he can claim that his fulsome recourse to the media follows a path traversed by many eminent predecessors.

Among the stars in Nasar's firmament, none shines as brightly as Keynes. Five of the eighteen chapters in *Grand Pursuit* are devoted principally if not wholly to Keynes, while three chapters principally focus on Schumpeter and two on Hayek.

Early in his career, Keynes concentrated on the role of money and its effect on prices, exchange rates, and trade. His later concerns shifted to employment and particularly to the high and sustained unemployment generated by the Great Depression. The link between his prior work on money and his later concern with unemployment led him to invent the concept of "aggregate demand" and, in particular, the insufficiency of aggregate demand (that is, consumer demand plus investors' demand) to generate full employment when recessions strike. The Keynesian remedy was a large expansion of deficit-financed government spending to boost aggregate demand. Furthermore, the effectiveness of this remedy was said to be hugely enhanced by the elixir of the so-called multiplier—hopefully calculated as the sum of a geometric progression whose first term is the proportion of incremental government spending spent by the initial recipients of that spending and whose second, third, and subsequent terms comprise the same proportion spent by these latter and continuing recipients, ad infinitum.

Elixir indeed! As I mentioned earlier in this review, empirical work has been done by thoroughly competent economists (Barro and Boskin, neither of whom is mentioned in *Grand Pursuit*) showing that the effects of deficit-financed government spending on aggregate demand and on employment have either been negligible or negative in prior recessions and in the recent recession of 2007–2008. The absence of empirical support for the Keynesian remedy and its multiplier elixir suggests that there may well be flaws in the underlying theory.

For many economists, flawed theory would be of greater concern—at least more hurtful to professional pride—than nugatory results from stimulus programs based on a valid theory. Moreover, indications of a flawed theory signify that no amount of improvements in program design would be likely to help. Although not addressed by Nasar, a brief summary of flaws in the Keynesian theory follows.[1]

Central to the Keynesian theory of deficit-financed government spending and the multiplier concept associated with it is the assumption that the admittedly insufficient level of consumer and investment demand experienced during a recession would not be further depressed as a consequence of the added government borrowing. In a theory that purported to be "general" (i.e., Keynes's major work is *The General Theory of Employment, Interest, and Money*) rather than a singular, "special" case, this is a strong and vulnerable assumption. In theory, as well as in fact, the levels of spending by consumers and investors that prevail prior to and during a recession might actually be further reduced as a response to the debt-financed additional dose of government spending. There are three plausible reasons for this response:

1. "Ricardian equivalence" is a conjecture advanced by David Ricardo suggesting that consumers and investors might reduce their spending to prepare for the tax increases they would face in the future in order to pay for the added government spending financed by borrowing in the present. Ricardo's idea was formulated a century before Keynes's general theory and thus was something Keynes should have been aware of.

2. Friedman's "permanent income" hypothesis suggested that spending by consumers depended on their expected permanent income and would be unaffected by any windfall increases in income they regarded as temporary or at most that any increases in consumption that might result would be slight.

3. Investors' spending might shrink as a result of increased government spending because of anticipated increases in future taxes, or because of increased regulatory restrictions attached to the government spending, or simply because

investment alternatives abroad might appear to be less onerous and more profitable.

Grand Pursuit has an ambitiously wide reach that sometimes
exceeds its grasp. Yet it is a good read—a quality that reflects its
author's credentials as a journalist (rarely do economists write as
well as Nasar). That said, I have reservations about her choice of
a subtitle, *The Story of Economic Genius.* I'm familiar with the work
of all the economists whom she discusses, and I've been person-
ally acquainted with several of them, either as my graduate school
professors or as colleagues. All were very smart; none qualifies for
admission to the genius category. Perhaps the single economist
who *would* qualify is one who receives only passing acknowledg-
ment by Nasar but who inhabited an earlier period than her book
is concerned with: Adam Smith.

Note

1. A more extended treatment of the topic is contained in
Chapter 12.

POSTAUDIT

Sylvia Nasar's review of the pantheon of economics' luminaries is a delightful read while also reflecting something of the
author's own likes and lesser likes. *Score: Good*

About the Author

Charles Wolf Jr. holds the distinguished chair in international economics at RAND. He is a professor of policy analysis in the Pardee RAND Graduate School, and he received his BS and PhD degrees in economics from Harvard. From 1967 until June 1981, he was head of RAND's Economics Department, and thereafter was director of RAND research in international economics. He was the founding dean of the RAND Graduate School, serving in that capacity from 1970 to 1997.

Dr. Wolf is a senior research fellow at the Hoover Institution, and he was a director of Capital Income Builder Fund Inc. and Capital World Growth and Income Fund Inc. from 1986 through 2010. He has served with the Department of State and has taught at Cornell, the University of California at Berkeley, UCLA, and Nuffield College, Oxford. He is the author of more than 250 journal articles and the author or coauthor of two dozen books including *Foreign Aid: Theory and Practice in Southern Asia (1960)*, *Rebellion and Authority: An Analytic Essay on Insurgent Conflicts (1970)*, *The Costs of the Soviet Empire (1986)*, *Markets or Governments: Choosing Between Imperfect Alternatives (1993)*, *Asian Economic Trends and Their Security Implications (2000)*, *Fault Lines in China's Economic Terrain (2003)*, *Looking Backward and Forward: Policy Issues in the 21st Century (2008)*, *China and India, 2025: A Comparative Assessment (2011)*,

China's Expanding Role in Global Mergers and Acquisitions Markets (2011), and *China's Foreign Aid and Government-Sponsored Investment Activities (2013)*. He is a frequent contributor to the *Wall Street Journal*, the *Wall Street Journal Asia*, the *Wall Street Journal Europe*, the *Weekly Standard*, and the *International Economy*.

In 2007, Wolf received the Order of the Rising Sun, Japan's highest honor for academic attainment. The ceremony was held at the Foreign Ministry in Tokyo, followed by a reception with Emperor Akihito at the Imperial Palace.

Index

Fund (IMF) economic study for,
174–175; international organizations, economic studies by, 173–
175; interpretation of pooled economic studies, 177–178; investment
rate of economies and estimates
for, 171–172; invitations to join
PSI, 221–222; Iran, transactions
with, 218; labor-intensive manufacturing, emphasis on, 179;
McKinsey Global Institute estimates
for, 173; neoclassical model for
economic forecasts, 168, 169, 170;
North Korea, transactions with,
218; one-child policy, 8, 46, 167;
optimistic economic forecasts for,
178; per capita income estimates
by Goldman Sachs study, 171;
process for meta-analysis, 183–184;
qualitative factors affecting performance by, 183; savings rates in,
22, 44–46, 63, 139–140; Shanghai
Cooperation Organisation, 217;
sources for meta-analysis of, 183–
184; summary of pooled economic
studies, 176–177; uncertainty of
economic forecasts, 175–180;
World Bank economic assessment for, 174. *See also* Chinese
Communist Party; FAGIA
(foreign aid and government-
sponsored investment activities);
foreign investments by China;
People's Liberation Army, China;
Proliferation Security Initiative
(PSI); yuan
China-Africa Development Fund, 6;
FAGIA and, 26–27
China Development Bank, 5; FAGIA
loans from, 26–27; foreign aid
loans from, 34
China National Offshore Oil
Corporation, 27, 66
China Petroleum Company
(Sinopec), 27, 66

Chinese Communist Party, 3–5; corruption affecting, 76–77; domestic
consumption, encouragement of,
62; dual-track price system and, 73;
FAGIA, management of, 27; private
sector activity and, 39; propelling
growth agenda of, 72; rule of law
and, 39
Chongqing model of economic development, 77, 134
Chow, Brian G., 9–19, 215–223
Churchill, Winston, 161, 202
class paradox of China, 3–5
class warfare: inequality and, 133,
233–234; US, debate in, 102
CNOOC (China National Offshore
Oil Corporation), 23
Coase, Ronald, 37–40
Coase theorem, 37
Cobb-Douglas production functions,
162
communism, 3–5. *See also* Chinese
Communist Party
Confucion Institutes, 35
Confucius, 55
consumer credit: in China, 50–51, 63;
in US, 51
Consumer Financial Protection
Bureau, US, 51
consumption: China, increasing
domestic consumption in, 50–51,
59, 61–64, 146; debt-financed government spending and, 90; prior
consumption demand, 85
consumption demand, 83
copper: China's investments in, 15;
US exports, 119
corruption: actual rate of corruption
(ARC), 74; anticorruption efforts
in China, 74; Chinese Communist
Party and, 76–77; Chongqing
model of development, 77; cumulative level of corruption (CLC),
74; degenerative corruption, 71,
72; developmental corruption in